The Education and Training of Personnel Involved in the Handling and Monitoring of Hazardous Wastes

EF/92/05/EN

European Foundation
for the Improvement of
Living and Working Conditions

The Education and Training of Personnel Involved in the Handling and Monitoring of Hazardous Wastes

by
Richard Haines
and
Duncan Bardsley

Ecotec
Research and Consulting Ltd

Birmingham, United Kingdom
Brussels, Belgium
June 1991

Loughlinstown House, Shankill, Co. Dublin, Ireland
Tel: 282 68 88 Fax: 282 64 56 Telex: 30726 EURF EI

Cataloguing data can be found at the end of this publication

Luxembourg: Office of Official Publications of the European
 Communities, 1992

ISBN 92-826-3998-3

© European Foundation for the Improvement of Living and Working Conditions, 1992. For rights of translation or reproduction, applications should be made to the Director, European Foundation for the Improvement of Living and Working Conditions, Loughlinstown House, Shankill, Co. Dublin, Ireland.

Printed in Ireland

PREFACE

The Foundation's activities regarding hazardous wastes date back to 1984 when, at the request of the European Parliament, it commissioned a series of studies on the Legal, Technical and Safety Aspects relating to the Transport of Dangerous Wastes. These studies were undertaken in support of the Commission's implementation of the Council Directive (84/631/EEC) on the supervision and control within the European Community of the transfrontier shipments of hazardous wastes.

The definition of the further work of the Foundation, within the framework of its four-year programme 1985-1988, was based on the discussions at a European Round Table on Safety Aspects of Hazardous Wastes which took place in November 1985. It examined the existing and future problems in this field, brought forward new ideas and pointed in its conclusions and recommendations to a considerable number of areas where action by the Foundation and the Community institutions, notably the Commission, was required.

As a follow-up to the Round Table, a series of studies were undertaken regarding Contaminated Land in the European Community (1985-86), Safety Aspects relating to the Handling and Monitoring of Hazardous Wastes (1986-87), Hazardous Wastes and the Public (1987-88) and Education and Training relating to Hazardous Wastes (1988-89). The studies on Safety Aspects relating to the Handling and Monitoring of Hazardous Wastes revealed a number of shortcomings of the existing national legislation, Community directives and practices aimed at both work-safety and environmental protection in this area, and of the internal safety procedures at establishments handling hazardous wastes. They also confirmed one of the conclusions from the Round Table, i.e. that poor waste management was often the result of inadequate training of the personnel working in this field. The studies on Education and Training relating to Hazardous Wastes, which were subsequently carried out in all Member States in 1988-89, examined, in detail, the existing legislation, procedures and practices, as well as the gaps and needs, regarding the training provision for all categories of personnel working at hazardous waste facilities, at regulatory agencies and in the emergency services or involved in the transportation of hazardous wastes or in the clean-up of contaminated soil.

This report brings together the findings of the twelve national studies and analyses them in the wider European Community context. It examines the extent to which the existing measures, procedures and practices are adequate, and it points to a considerable number of shortcomings. Based on the national studies, the report also makes a number of recommendations aimed at filling the gaps in the existing training provision and at ensuring better practices and higher education and training standards in this area throughout the Community.

Following the completion of this report, a meeting was held in Brussels, on 25 April 1990, to enable representatives of the employers, trade unions, governments and the Commission of the European Communities - the constituent bodies of the Foundation's Administrative Board - to evaluate the findings of the research. The participants agreed on the value of the work carried out and on the quality and usefulness of the present report. They pointed to the need for an inventory of contaminated sites in the Community, but recognised that it would be a medium- or long-term task owing to the insufficient information in some Member States and the different methods applied. They also recommended that environmental education and training be strengthened throughout the educational system, and that a major effort be made towards increasing environmental awareness among consumers and manufacturers. The Commission's initiative on eco-labelling was seen as a positive step in this respect. Moreover, the participants pointed out that public authorities in charge of training and advising the personnel of local councils and contractors on waste management might also be able to advise small and medium-size enterprises on the same issue. A few minor amendments suggested at the evaluation meeting have been included in the report.

The Foundation's work on hazardous wastes 1984-89 has been followed up by the preparation of a comprehensive report on Hazardous Waste Management in the European Community which is scheduled for publication in late 1992.

Jørn Pedersen
Dublin, February 1992

ACKNOWLEDGEMENTS

This report presents a synthesis of the key finding of twelve national studies on the Education and Training of Personnel Involved in the Handling and Monitoring of Hazardous Wastes in the European Community. These studies were commissioned by the European Foundation for the Improvement of Living and Working Conditions and were carried out in 1987-88.

ECOTEC Research and Consulting Ltd would like to acknowledge the valuable input the project has had from the following individuals and organisations who prepared the national reports which provided the information synthesised in this report.

Belgium	Ms Marie Hannequart
Denmark	Mr Mogens Polmark ENVIROPLAN
Federal Republic of Germany	Josef Noeke Jorn Timm INFU
France	Rene Goubier ANRED
Greece	ECOTEC Research and Consulting Ltd
Ireland	Dr J A Kearney EOLAS
Italy	Dr G U Fortunati
Luxembourg	Ms Marie Hannequart
Netherlands	H S Buijtenhek G J Kremers J P L M van der Velden TAUW CONSULT bv
Portugal	Mr Martins Reis TECNINVEST sa
Spain	TREISA sa
United Kingdom	Dr R C Haines Mr D A Bardsley ECOTEC Research and Consulting Ltd

Contents

1.0 INTRODUCTION   12

  1.1 Background and Rationale for the Study 12
  1.2 Aims of the Studies 13
  1.3 Hazardous Waste in Europe 13
  1.4 Statutory Requirements Concerning the Education and Training of
       Personnel Involved in Hazardous Waste Management. 22
  1.5 Educational Programmes and Courses Provided for Those Working in the Sphere of
       Hazardous Waste Management 25

**2.0 EDUCATION AND TRAINING OF PERSONNEL WORKING AT HAZARDOUS
WASTE FACILITIES**   29

  2.1 Background of Personnel Involved in the Handling and Treatment of
       Hazardous Wastes 29
  2.2 Existing Training Provision 32
  2.3 Gaps and Needs in the Existing Training Provision 37
  2.4 Conclusions and Recommendations 37

**3.0 EDUCATION AND TRAINING OF PERSONNEL INVOLVED IN THE
TRANSPORTATION OF HAZARDOUS WASTES**   41

  3.1 Road Transport 41
  3.2 Rail Transport 45
  3.3 Sea Transport 46
  3.4 Transport by Inland Waterways 47
  3.5 Conclusions and recommendations 48

**4.0 EDUCATION AND TRAINING OF PERSONNEL INVOLVED IN THE
CLEAN-UP OF CONTAMINATED SOIL**   51

  4.1 The Approach to the Problem 51
  4.2 Background of Personnel Involved 52
  4.3 Existing Training Provision 53
  4.4 Gaps and Needs in the Existing Training Provision 54
  4.5 Conclusions and Recommendations 54

**5.0 EDUCATION AND TRAINING IN RELATION TO THE DUTIES AND
RESPONSIBILITIES OF REGULATORY AGENCIES**   57

    5.1 Introduction 57
    5.2 Responsible Bodies 57
    5.3 Background of Personnel Involved 60
    5.4 Existing Training Provision 62
    5.6 Conclusions and Recommendations 66

**6.0 EDUCATION AND TRAINING OF THOSE IN THE EMERGENCY
SERVICES IN RELATION TO HAZARDOUS WASTE**   67

    6.1 Integration of the Emergency Services in Relation to Hazardous Waste 67
    6.2 Medical, Nursing and Paramedical Staff 67
    6.3 Fire Brigade 68
    6.4 Police 70
    6.5 Civil Defence Organisations 71
    6.6 Conclusions and Recommendations 72

7.0 CONCLUSIONS AND RECOMMENDATIONS   73

    7.1 Introduction 73
    7.2 Findings of the study 73
    7.3 Recommendations 77

LIST OF TABLES AND ANNEXES

Table 1.1	Variability of Hazardous Waste Definitions used by Member States	16
Table 1.2	Hazardous Waste Arisings : Principal Sources and Disposal Routes	18
Annex I	Examples of Courses and Agencies Providing Training on Aspects of Hazardous Waste Management	79

1.0 INTRODUCTION

1.1 Background and Rationale for the Study

In November 1985, the European Foundation for the Improvement of Living and Working Conditions held a European Round Table on Safety Aspects of Hazardous Wastes. The purpose of the Round Table was to guide the Foundation in defining its research on this theme as part of a four-year rolling programme 1985-1988.

A series of recommendations formed part of a research agenda. Several of these recommendations focused on the provisions and measures required to ensure the safe handling and monitoring of hazardous wastes in the European Community (EC), particularly at waste disposal sites and waste treatment plants. In 1986-87, studies were carried out in the twelve Member States and summarised in the consolidated report 'A Study on the Safety Aspects Relating to the Handling and Monitoring of Hazardous Wastes'.

Other recommendations from the Round Table focused in particular on the need for adequate education and training of all personnel involved in the handling and management of hazardous wastes, whether management or operatives. The Round Table suggested that the research programme should include:

- the evaluation of existing education and training procedures and programmes and the implementation of any improvements required;

- an investigation into the feasibility of introducing harmonised curricula on a Community basis;

- a study both of the training needs of medical personnel (e.g. general practitioners, public health officials and employment medical services) in identifying the effects of exposure to chemicals, and of the ways in which this training might be provided.

The recommendations of the Round Table are also closely related to a number of other studies carried out by the Foundation. Examples include the Transportation of Toxic and Dangerous Wastes (carried out in 1984-1985), a 1986 project on contaminated land in the EC (undertaken in co-operation with the German Federal Ministry for Research and Technology and the Commission) and a study on Hazardous Wastes and the Public (undertaken in 1987).

The above-mentioned studies reflect the concern expressed by certain Community institutions, particularly the Commission and the European Parliament, as to the adequacy of certain procedures, measures and practices regarding hazardous wastes management. They have been, or are being, undertaken in support of Community policies, and there is a close connection between the present study and the activities on information and education relating to waste management mentioned in the Community's Fourth Environmental Action Programme 1987-1992.

In the light of the above, a study on The Education and Training of Personnel involved in the Handling and Monitoring of Hazardous Wastes was undertaken in all Member States. Its purpose was to provide a detailed analysis of existing training provision, to identify the gaps and needs, and to put forward appropriate recommendations. A synthesis of the key findings of these studies is presented in this report. Plans also exist to prepare a consolidated report of the findings of all the European Foundation research in this area.

1.2 Aims of the Studies

The aims of the studies undertaken in all Member States were:

- to provide the Foundation, the Community institutions, Member States, relevant local authorities and social partners with a comprehensive picture and a comparative analysis of existing and planned education and training facilities in relation to hazardous wastes;
- to identify and analyse the educational and training needs of specific categories of personnel and of professionals dealing with problems relating to hazardous wastes, and to illustrate present shortcomings;
- to review successful training programmes and to encourage better and more extensive educational and training schemes for all relevant personnel both by pointing to improvements and by the exchange of information;
- to identify ways of improving both safety standards and possible remedial action in relation to hazardous wastes.

The national reports closely followed a set of guidelines drawn up by the Foundation. These guidelines set out the information to be obtained and the analysis to be undertaken. The work was guided by a co-ordination group of experts and representatives of the Commission, trade unions, employers and the Foundation's Committee of Experts.

The remaining paragraphs of Section 1 of the report place the education and training of personnel involved in hazardous waste management within the EC context of hazardous waste arisings and the relevant statutory education and training requirements.

Sections 2.0 to 6.0 summarise the education and training of personnel working in hazardous waste facilities, in the transportation of hazardous wastes, in the clean-up of contaminated soil, in regulatory agencies and in the emergency services, respectively.

The final section of the report brings together the findings and conclusions of each section and presents recommendations concerning the education and training of those involved in all aspects of the management of hazardous wastes.

1.3 Hazardous Waste in Europe

1.3.1 Community and National Definitions of Hazardous Wastes

In terms of Community legislation, the Framework Directive on waste, 75/442/EEC, places a general duty on Member States to take the necessary measures to ensure that waste is disposed of without endangering human health and without harming the environment. Although certain categories are excluded from the scope of the Directive, 'waste' is defined as:

'all materials which contain, or remain after the use of, and which cannot be considered to be by-products, whose holder intends or needs to dispose of them'.

A subsequent Directive on toxic and dangerous waste, 78/319/EEC, provides the following definition of 'toxic and dangerous waste':

'any waste containing or contaminated by the substances or materials listed in the Annex to this Directive of such a nature, in such quantities or in such concentrations as to constitute a risk to health and the environment'.

The Annex lists 27 substances and the Directive specifies wastes that are to be excluded such as radioactive waste, explosives and hospital waste.

The Directive places a general duty on Member States to ensure that toxic and dangerous waste is disposed of without harming human health or the environment, and its main provision is that toxic and dangerous waste may be stored, treated and/or deposited only by authorised undertakings. It also makes provision for plans to be made, records to be kept, transport controlled, inspections made and reports produced.

The notification date of this Directive was 22 March, 1978, with normal compliance due on 22 March, 1980. For some Member States this has caused few difficulties as national legislation covering both general aspects of toxic and dangerous wastes and the framework Directive were already in place. Some Member States, however, have still not fully implemented the Directive.

Some of the difficulties in compliance are due largely to the imprecision of the definition of toxic and dangerous waste contained in the Directive. This has resulted in a broad interpretation and a variety of working definitions within the EC.

In some Member States, the issue of compliance with the Directive itself is confused by the ambiguities and interpretations of national toxic and dangerous waste definitions. For example, the UK defines toxic and dangerous wastes (special wastes) as those wastes dangerous to human health, omitting from the definition references to wastes that may be damaging to the environment. However, the Directive clearly states that the definition should include substances that constitute a risk to the environment. Some Member States have difficulty where strong regional administrations (such as in Belgium and Germany) have independently drawn up their own definitions of toxic and hazardous waste.

Whereas in some Member States full compliance with the letter and spirit of the Directive's definition is in doubt, others implement a toxic and dangerous waste definition that is far more comprehensive than that of the Directive. In Denmark, for example, 51 types of hazardous waste are defined, and a classification system based on industry source is also operated. The Spanish definition, although based on the Directive has extended the provisions by including two additional substances to the 27 listed in the Directive, by having a more limited list of excluded wastes, and by including within the scope of its law those empty containers that have been used to hold wastes. Furthermore, lists have also been produced which define the generic type, constituents and characteristics of hazardous wastes and the industrial processes that generate them. In Italy, concentrations of certain hazardous substances, a list of hazardous waste producing activities and a list of defined substances are all parameters used to define hazardous wastes. Various other definitions are operated within the EC, and a comparative summary of each of the national definitions is given in Table 1.1.

The following discussion groups together those Member States which operate similar toxic waste definitions. It should be noted, however, that the terminology used by Member States varies, and terms such as chemical waste, special waste, special industrial waste and hazardous waste are, in the context of this report, equivalent to 'toxic and dangerous waste' as specified in Directive 78/319/EEC.

At the simplest level, Portugal and Greece use the toxic and dangerous waste definition of Directive 78/319/EEC. They have not expanded the list of dangerous substances contained in Annex I of that Directive, nor have they introduced any concentration criteria, though in Portugal the concept of hazardous waste is under review in order to bring it into line with the definition offered by the OECD in it's Draft Decision on Monitoring the Transfrontier Shipment of Hazardous Wastes. The definitions used in the remaining ten Member States vary significantly. Ireland has no hazardous waste definition formally incorporated into national law but interprets the Directive's definition in its widest sense. Other Member States make extensive use of the physical and chemical properties of waste to establish a legal classification of wastes as dangerous or hazardous. Others have, as mentioned above, extended the substances list and have specified both concentration criteria and hazardous waste producing processes.

Although the legal definitions used by Member States may affect the operational practice of sampling, monitoring and disposal of such wastes, the stringency or precision of definition does not necessarily ensure either good control in hazardous waste management or that all hazardous wastes are covered by the definition and thus by the requirements of the legislation. In Italy, for example, substances and waste-producing industrial processes are used to define hazardous waste. However, such a system calls for a considerable degree of analytical testing which can result in delays and higher treatment and disposal costs.

On the other hand the lack of a national definition in Ireland has not inhibited control. There are several laws relating to the disposal of waste and a non-legal memorandum, issued by the Irish Department of the Environment, has been generally adopted and implemented by industry as a quasi-legal document. The memorandum includes an extensive list of types of waste to which local authorities refer when determining if a waste is toxic and dangerous. Furthermore, it is not necessarily required that one or more of the 27 substances of the Directive be present. In addition, the list of wastes contained in the memorandum is not, in practice, considered to be exhaustive. Local authorities can independently designate other wastes as toxic or dangerous that are not contained on the list.

Thus the lack of rigid legislative control and definition can allow control authorities to adopt a wide interpretation, in some cases tighter than that given by Directive 78/319/EEC. Other definitions, however, that appear precise and unambiguous can, when put into practice, be narrow in scope and limited in effect. For example, the specification of a concentration value (g/kg) may have no regard to the effect of the total quantity of waste being disposed of. Thus, although a substance concentration may be below the threshold and, under the terms of the definition, non-hazardous, the total waste load may contain a substantial quantity of the contaminating material and be capable of causing considerable environmental damage.

While the foregoing definitions are related to Directive 78/319/EEC, a new proposal for a Council Directive on hazardous waste was issued in November 1988 (88/C295/04). This proposed Directive has taken into account the experience gained in the implementation of the Toxic and Dangerous Waste Directive (78/319/EEC) and seeks to introduce a new definition of hazardous waste which lists the generic types of hazardous waste, together with the waste constituents and characteristics which render them hazardous. In the light of this proposed new Directive consideration is being given to the UK definition of 'special waste'. It is envisaged that, once the new Directive has been adopted, the current UK definition will be amended to include criteria concerned with environmental damage and pollution risk.

TABLE 1.1 : VARIABILITY OF HAZARDOUS WASTE DEFINITIONS USED BY MEMBER STATES

Country	Extended List of Annex 1 78/319/EEC	Defines Physical & Chemical Criteria for Hazardous Waste	Defines the Concentration Criteria of Substances	Defines Haz. Waste Production Processes	Regional Variations in Definition or Interpretation
Belgium	*	*	*	*	■
Denmark	■	■	*	■	*
France	■	*	*	■	*
Germany	*	*	*	■	■
Greece	*	*	*	*	*
Ireland	■	*	*	■	■
Italy	■	*	■	■	■
Luxembourg	■	*	■	*	■
Netherlands	■	*	■	■	*
Portugal	■	*	*	*	*
Spain	■	■	■	■	*
UK	*	■	*	*	*

■   Indicates adoption of this aspect into the national definitions

1.3.2 Arisings of Hazardous Waste in the Community and Their Treatment or Disposal

The bulk of toxic and dangerous wastes are generated by the process industries, the main producers being the chemicals sector and the mineral and metal producing industries. Other industrial sectors, laboratories and hospitals also produce significant quantities. These wastes can arise as unwanted by-products through cleansing processes and from waste treatment or recovery processes, or they may result from accidents or spillages. They can occur as relatively pure substances or as complex mixtures: quantities may be small or large and may be in the form of gases, liquids, slurries or solids.

Although the legislation requires the competent authorities of Member States to keep records of the quantity, nature, physical and chemical characteristics and origin of waste, the data are not of uniform quality throughout the EC.

Several factors affect the accuracy of the data on hazardous waste arisings. These include:

- the wide variation in national definitions used;
- reluctance by industry to supply data;
- poor data collection methods and infrequency of data collection;
- the degree to which 'hazardous waste' is 'hidden' by industry and not therefore recognised as such by the competent authorities.

Variations in the definition of hazardous waste used in Member States result in the data rarely being comparable between States. In Portugal, for instance, a recent inventory of toxic and dangerous waste used a much broader concept of the definition than that provided by Directive 78/319/EEC. Based on this broader concept, it is estimated that 1 million tonnes of toxic waste is generated every year by various industrial processes in Portugal. By 1995 this figure is forecast to rise to 2.2 million tonnes, not only because of growth in manufacturing sectors but also as a result of new restrictions on uncontrolled discharges of industrial liquid effluent. At present the bulk of hazardous wastes produced in Portugal is in the chemical sector which is responsible for 80% of all hazardous wastes generated.

In France it is estimated that, using the definitions contained in the latest draft Community Directive, some 4 million tonnes of dangerous industrial wastes are generated each year (out of a total of 18 million tonnes of special waste).

In the UK, 'special waste' arisings (equatable to 'toxic and dangerous waste') amounted in 1986 to a little over 1.6 million tonnes. However, it is estimated that under the broader definition of hazardous or notifiable wastes, 3.7 million tonnes arose in England alone for disposal in 1986.

Under the more precise definition used in the Netherlands, where toxic and dangerous wastes are specified by the concentration of certain toxic substances and/or by the industrial process from which they emanate, it is estimated that 1 million tonnes of chemical waste are generated each year.

Some attempt has been made to summarise the figures for hazardous waste arisings in Table 1.2. It should be noted that this table is based not only on different definitions, as exemplified above, but also on figures for different years. Caution is therefore required when making comparisons.

TABLE 1.2 : HAZARDOUS WASTE ARISINGS - PRINCIPAL SOURCES AND DISPOSAL ROUTES

Country	Quantity of Toxic and Dangerous Wastes '000s tonnes	Year	Principal Sources or Types of Waste	Principal Disposal Routes
Belgium	1000	1987	Cleaning wastes, sludges, mixed organics and inorganics	Landfill treatment, and incineration
Denmark	150	1988	Oil wastes and organic chemical waste	Physical, chemical treatment and incineration
France	4000	1988	Organic chemical and mineral wastes	Landfill, incineration and treatment
Germany	5500	1987	Sulphur containing waste, acids, solvents and sludges	Landfill (31%), dumping at sea (18%), incineration (8%), treatment (7%)
Greece	*	*	Sludges and liquid effluent	Landfill (90%) (new specialist treatment/disposal capacity is planned
Luxembourg		1986	Organic wastes, flammable substances, and acids	Landfill
Ireland	58	1984	Organic and chlorinated plants, lead compounds, asbestos and acids	Export (for treatment and disposal - 28%), on-site treatment (66%), including recycling and incineration
Italy	2000	1984	Manufacturing industry	Landfill and incineration
Netherlands	1000	1985	Chemical, petrochemicals and metals industry	Treated (in-house) (55%), incineration (10%), treated/recycled (20%), controlled landfill (5%), export (10%)
Portugal	1050	1987	Chemical tanneries, pulp and paper, iron and steel industries	Uncontrolled landfill (new specialist treatment/disposal capacity is planned)**
Spain	1800	1988	Chemical, pulp and paper and metal processing industries	Uncontrolled landfill (93%) incineration, treatment recycling (7%) (new specialist treatment/disposal capacity is planned)
UK	1610	1986	Manufacturing industry	landfill (79%)
Approx Total	**18146 tonnes**			

* *No data available*

** Note that the definition of controlled landfill is not consistent throughout Member States and what is regarded as controlled in one State may not necessarily be acceptable in another. Therefore, where landfill is indicated in the above table, the reader should not make any qualitative conclusions or comparison regarding the standards of landfill disposal within each Member State.

To put the arisings of hazardous waste into context, it is currently estimated that the total arisings of all wastes in the EC is some 2,200 million tonnes per year, 160 million tonnes of which comprise industrial waste. Thus arisings of hazardous waste account for approximately 0.8% of all EC waste and some 11% of industrial waste.

If the broader definition of toxic and hazardous waste were to be used throughout the EC, total arisings would be some 70-80 million tonnes per year, or approximately 50% of industrial waste arisings. This would be likely to create major difficulties for waste disposal concerns with inadequate capacity and for the responsible monitoring authorities, and would be likely to lead to a greater degree of inappropriate disposal than is currently the case.

Data collection procedures and the frequency of data collection also show considerable variation between Member States. In the UK there has been no systematic survey of waste arisings and the figures produced are based on annual estimates made by the Hazardous Waste Inspectorate. Similarly, in Greece, there is no centralised operational procedure for collecting data of this kind.

Even where inventories have been made, the figures are frequently out of date or unreliable. In Spain, for example, comprehensive figures for arisings were compiled in 1981. Since then, several of the Autonomous Communities in Spain have drawn up their own inventories, but these are not considered to be reliable, either because of the financial and time constraints imposed on their compilation or because industries have been unwilling to supply the appropriate information. The most recent estimation of arisings (Direccion General del Medio Ambiento) of toxic and dangerous waste for 1988 is 1.8 million tonnes.

The accuracy of information is also affected by measurement problems. In some countries the units of measurement are not comparable or convertible. In the UK and Ireland, for example, waste loads may be recorded in tonnes, litres, skipfulls, lorry loads, drums or tanker loads. Of these units, few have established magnitudes, and significant errors can occur when compiling total waste quantities.

Data on arisings can originate from a number of different sources. These include notifications provided by waste producing authorities, questionnaires provided by industry and records kept by waste producing companies. The value of the data in compiling national statistics depends on the degree of coverage and on the accuracy of the information supplied.

Some countries have systems which facilitate the collection and compilation of waste arisings. In France, the intention is to introduce computerised monitoring. In Denmark, industries producing chemical wastes are required to notify the relevant municipality of the quantity of arisings. In most Member States, despite the requirement of the toxic waste Directive 78/319/EEC that records be kept, an appropriate system of record keeping has not been established, and inventories are the only means of assessing the total quantities of waste produced.

The principal disposal routes for hazardous wastes are also shown in Table 1.2 and include landfill, physical and chemical treatment and incineration. There is considerable variation in disposal practices within the EC. For example, in Denmark, the majority of wastes are either treated or incinerated at one central plant, KOMMUNEKEMI, whereas, in the UK, 79% of hazardous waste is co-disposed directly to controlled landfill. In France, a variety of disposal methods are used, including landfill, incineration, treatment and recycling.

This variation in disposal routes between Member States arises for several reasons. These include:

- national policies on waste management;
- the availability of sites and facilities for disposal;
- hydrogeological and other physical factors;
- the influence of industry and the costs of disposal;
- the influence of environmental protection lobby groups;
- the quantity of arisings.

In the EC as a whole, landfilling remains the predominant disposal route, whether by co-disposal or by controlled or uncontrolled tipping methods. However, the information available suggests that the proportion of hazardous waste disposed of in this way will decrease, particularly as countries such as Spain, Portugal and Greece implement their plans for new treatment plant.

1.3.3 Number of Hazardous Waste Facilities

The number of hazardous waste facilities in operation varies between the Member States. The reasons for this variation include such factors as the degree of industrialisation, the degree of government control, and the level of environmental concern.

Denmark and Luxembourg have each responded to the problem of relatively limited quantities of toxic waste by concentrating handling and processing in the hands of a single organisation. In Denmark, apart from a small number of companies involved in the recycling of solvents and other chemicals, all toxic wastes are processed by KOMMUNEKEMI, a municipally owned central treatment plant. The Societe Lamesch, located at Steinsel near the city of Luxembourg, was originally involved exclusively in the management and recycling of household, industrial and commercial waste. Since 1982, however, it has become involved in the collection, transport, treatment and disposal of toxic and dangerous wastes. A few approved foreign collectors of toxic and dangerous wastes also operate in Luxembourg.

In Greece, Spain and Portugal, the main method of waste disposal is by landfill, much of it uncontrolled tipping. In Portugal a few enterprises in the chemicals sector (refineries and producers of basic organic chemicals, man-made fibres and synthetic resins) incinerate toxic wastes, mainly in the form of organic sludges. Some recycling also takes place. In Spain, public facilities are restricted to a physical/chemical treatment plant and a controlled landfill site, each capable of handling 20,000 tonnes of hazardous wastes per year, and both located near Madrid. Other companies located in the vicinity of Madrid, Barcelona and Vizcaya specialise in such activities as the recovery of used oils, the distillation of organic solvents, the neutralisation of acid and basic solutions, solidification processes and the rendering of wastes inert.

In other Member States, the number of hazardous waste treatment facilities is considerable. Of some 5,200 licensed disposal facilities in the UK, 1,600 are licensed to receive some form of hazardous waste. Of these, 1,150 are landfill sites, the remainder comprising transfer stations, incinerators and treatment facilities. The quantities of hazardous waste received by many of these facilities are very small and only a few are permitted to receive or treat 'special' wastes.

Belgium, France, Germany and the Netherlands operate various types of facility. In the Netherlands, concern over groundwater contamination severely limits the amount of landfill permitted, and the emphasis is on storage and eventual treatment of chemical wastes in incinerators or physical/chemical treatment plants. Some 258 official local authority depots exist whose operators collect and store chemical waste, eventually disposing of it to waste processors. Furthermore, apart from the large number of companies that treat their own chemical waste and do not require a Chemical Waste Act permit, there are around 400 holders of such permits who process permitted categories of waste.

In France, in addition to 11 controlled landfill sites, 12 incineration plants and seven physical/chemical treatment works, no less than 10 cement works in various parts of the country have been adapted to burn industrial wastes. In addition, there are nine major waste facilities specialising in the treatment of soluble oils and/or water/hydrocarbon mixes.

In Germany, in 1988, there were believed to be 65 special waste dumps. Twenty-two companies offered an incineration service, including one ship, and 83 operators provided a physical/chemical treatment service.

1.3.4 Number of Contaminated Sites and the Magnitude of the Problem

Information concerning the number of contaminated sites varies considerably within the EC. The only Member State which does not experience problems as a result of land contamination is Ireland. This almost certainly reflects the relative youth of industry in Ireland, a country where large-scale industrial activity did not commence until the mid-1960s. Furthermore, there is no legacy of contaminated land arising from earlier economic activities.

In nearly every other Member State, however, land contamination poses some degree of threat to the public and to the environment. In Greece, Italy, Portugal and Spain, the lack of waste management and processing facilities has resulted in a high degree of uncontrolled tipping of wastes of all kinds. In Italy, for instance, the Inprat report, based on an investigation carried out by the Civil Protection Ministry, estimated that about 4,500 illegal dumps exist, many of them probably handling mixed or toxic wastes. Further details on the national situation should be available when the survey currently being carried out by the Castalia Company on behalf of the Environment Ministry has been completed.

No inventory of any kind exists in either Greece or Spain, but the number of contaminated sites is believed to be high. A Survey of Soil Contamination in Portugal identified 69 contaminated sites, 50% of them associated with tanneries in the Oporto and Santarem districts, but concluded that the total number of contaminated sites in the country was, in reality, very much higher.

No inventory of contaminated sites exists for either Belgium or Luxembourg, although in the former State soil contamination is recognised as a major problem. In the Netherlands, however, an inventory designed to establish the extent of the problem is being undertaken, based on provincial soil decontamination programmes.

The UK estimate of contaminated sites is 20,000, of which over 55% comprise disused gasworks. The 1982 Derelict Land Act allows various UK organisations to apply for a Derelict Land Grant to finance the reclamation or improvement of derelict land, including contaminated land. Of the 12 Member States, only the UK operates on the basis that public funds are a necessary requisite for the restoration of derelict land.

Information from the various provincial ministries of the Federal Republic of Germany estimated the number of identified or suspect sites at between 42,000 and 48,000, the largest concentrations occurring in North Rhine-Westphalia. This total is, however, likely to rise to between 60,000 and 70,000 as more detailed surveys are carried out.

It should be noted that the data provided above are for contaminated sites in general. It is not possible to offer conclusive information as to the degree of environmentally hazardous contamination involved, although a study of German provinces (excluding Schleswig-Holstein) did estimate that approximately one site in eight constituted a high potential hazard.

1.3.5 Hazardous Waste Transportation

The transportation of hazardous wastes within the EC is principally by road. Rail, ship and barge transport are also used but, in terms of the quantities transported, they are not significant. The dominance of road transportation results both from the nature of hazardous waste arisings and from the structure of the waste disposal industry. For example, the quantities of toxic and dangerous wastes produced by individual industries are often small in comparison to the quantities of non-hazardous waste produced. Their transportation is therefore only practicable and economic by road. Furthermore, road is often the only way of reaching many landfill sites, the location of which is more often determined by past mining activities than by transport considerations.

The degree of transportation varies from country to country. In Denmark, for instance, transportation is largely determined by access to KOMMUNEKEMI. The centralised nature of this planned facility has enabled a more even distribution of transport between road and rail. In Ireland, and to some extent Luxembourg, the need to export a proportion of hazardous wastes for processing abroad results in longer-distance international transportation involving, in the case of Ireland, ferry transport.

In more general terms, the more specialised the treatment method required for a particular waste, the greater the distance the waste will have to be transported, with all the implications for public and environmental safety that such transportation involves.

1.4 Statutory Requirements Concerning the Education and Training of Personnel Involved in Hazardous Waste Management.

1.4.1 General Regulations

Statutory regulations concerning the education and training of personnel involved in hazardous waste management are extremely limited in most Member States. There are very few stipulations as to the qualifications required, and most personnel are covered simply by the statutory regulations governing safety at work. These regulations usually include stipulations that employees must be made aware of the risks inherent in the work they do and that they must be instructed in appropriate safety measures.

In the UK, for example, the Health and Safety at Work Act, 1974 outlines the general duties concerning training which apply to all employers:

'It shall be the duty of every employer to ensure, so far as is reasonably practicable, the health, safety and welfare at work of his employees .... the matters to which that duty extends include ... the provision of such information, instruction, training and supervision ....'

More specific suggestions for training and other procedures to minimise risks to personnel may be made by Inspectors of the Health and Safety Executive during visits to waste disposal facilities.

In the Netherlands, the Working Conditions Act requires the guidance and instruction of employees on the nature of their work, on the hazards it entails and on how to avoid them. Provisions are laid down in the Safety Order for Factories and Places of Work (VBF), which comes under the scope of the Working

Conditions Act, that employees must be properly instructed in matters of safety at work, and that clear instructions must be given in the Dutch language.

In several countries, regulations do stipulate that those responsible for the management, handling and treatment of hazardous wastes must be properly qualified. It is rare for specific qualifications to be laid down, but it is usual for the various licensing authorities (as, for instance, in Ireland) to satisfy themselves that managers and supervisors at such facilities are properly qualified.

In Belgium, for instance, under the Law of 22 July, 1974 and the Walloon Regional Executive Order of 12 November, 1987, it is compulsory to place any operation involving the disposal of toxic or dangerous wastes under the authority of a responsible chemist who must have adequate experience in this field. Under the Regional Orders on controlled landfills (Flemish Executive Order of 21 April, 1982 and Walloon Regional Executive Order of 23 July, 1987) it is compulsory for acceptance and unloading/ decanting operations to be carried out under the supervision and in the presence of the operator or his representative. In the Walloon region, a responsible chemist is expressly responsible for the day-to-day supervision of operating conditions.

In Germany, the Waste Disposal Law similarly requires the staff in charge of waste disposal facilities to be properly qualified, and also stipulates that proper explanations be given to staff about the nature of their work and any possible hazards it entails. In the Netherlands, a recent draft Amendment to existing legislation states that persons working with hazardous materials must be expert in that type of work.

From the foregoing, it is apparent that most countries rely on existing legislation concerning health and safety at work, but that a number are becoming increasingly aware of the need for more specific legislation in relation to hazardous substances, including wastes.

1.4.2 Regulations Concerning the Education and Training of Those Involved in the Transportation of Hazardous Wastes

Road Transport

All road transport firms employing personnel are bound by their national regulations governing health and safety at work. There are, however, a number of other regulations in most Member States which relate to certain types of transportation. In several countries, for instance the UK, Denmark, Belgium, Luxembourg and the Netherlands, there are specific regulations concerning the training of tanker drivers, particularly where the containers are above a certain capacity (usually 3,000 litres) and where they are used to carry hazardous substances. For instance, in the Netherlands, since 1.1.88, all drivers engaged in either national or international transportation of dangerous substances in tanker bodies, tanks or multiple tanks with a total capacity of 3,000 litres or more must be in possession of either an international ADR professional training certificate for the Transportation of Dangerous Goods on the Highway, or of a CCV certificate for the Transportation of Dangerous Goods by Road.

In many countries, notably France, Germany, Ireland, Spain and Portugal, the regulations cover the transportation of any dangerous substance. In Ireland, for instance, drivers transporting any dangerous substance must receive training under the Dangerous Substances (Conveyance of Scheduled Substances by Road) (Trade or Business) Regulations of 1980. In Portugal, drivers of vehicles transporting dangerous goods must have a certificate verifying that they have successfully completed a training course relating to the specific safety requirements of the job. Germany, too, stipulates that only trained drivers may be entrusted with the transportation of hazardous substances and, in April 1988, the UK introduced statutory training for drivers of vehicles other than tankers which are used to carry dangerous substances.

However, in every instance quoted in the survey reports, these regulations relate to the carriage of hazardous substances in general, and there are no regulations specifically for hazardous wastes, which often involve mixes. In Denmark, obligatory special training for drivers transporting mixed cargoes of dangerous goods was considered and rejected. In the Netherlands, proper qualifications for the mixed transportation of dangerous goods are likely to become law by 1996.

Rail Transport

Rail transport is used to only a very limited degree for the transportation of hazardous wastes, and this is reflected in the information provided in the surveys. Belgium and the Netherlands simply comply with international regulations applying to the carriage of dangerous goods by rail, and relevant training is very limited, none of it being specifically oriented to the handling or management of hazardous wastes. In Germany, the regulations only indirectly apply minimum qualifications by stipulating that verification of the approval for forwarding hazardous goods must be carried out only by those familiar with the legal framework concerned and with the actual problems involved, and who are capable of putting this knowledge into practice.

Sea Transport

Only the surveys for Belgium, the Netherlands and Germany provided details of legislation concerning this method of transportation. In Belgium, maritime law is based on international convention which lays down certain regulations concerning the training of captains, officers, seamen and engineers of tanker vessels carrying chemical products or liquefied gases. The Dutch Shipping Decree lays down certain regulations for officer training where hazardous substances are being transported and, similarly, the German Hazardous Goods Decree, Sea Transport specifies certain safety obligations. Apart from these regulations, all of which relate to hazardous substances in general, there are no regulations for the training of those involved in the carriage of hazardous wastes at sea.

Transport on Inland Waterways

A similar situation obtains for transport on inland waterways. Apart from some Belgian legislation on wastes which lays down certain general safety obligations, there is no specific legislation concerning the training of those involved in the transportation of hazardous waste by inland waterway. Nearly all the regulations refer to hazardous substances in general. In Belgium, if a boat is to be used to transport hazardous substances, then the owner must possess certain certificates of approval. The main German and Dutch regulations concern the transportation of hazardous goods on the Rhine: the Netherlands now require everyone on board a ship sailing up and down the Rhine to have a valid ADNR certificate, while the main German regulation concerns the need to have a hazardous goods expert on board any ship carrying more than a certain quantity of specified hazardous goods.

1.5 Educational Programmes and Courses Provided for Those Working in the Sphere of Hazardous Waste Management

The range of educational programmes and courses on general offer to those working in the sphere of hazardous waste management varies greatly from one Member State to another. Greece, for instance, has no specific courses of this kind on offer, while countries such as Belgium and Denmark have a much more structured training programme involving a number of different institutions and including courses specifically linked to the management of hazardous compounds and partly hazardous wastes. The following paragraphs provide a very brief overview of some of the training opportunities in each Member State.

1.5.1 Belgium

Only the Centre for Study and Research on Safety, Ergonomics and the Promotion of Working Conditions (CRESEPT) offers specific external training in the management of hazardous substances and wastes. The courses offered are designed to familiarise safety managers, medical officers, chemists and engineers with the problems of managing hazardous substances and wastes. Various other bodies run relevant seminars, symposia and training days, and supplementary training courses are available for safety heads and deputies, and for health and workplace improvement departments.

Specific vocational courses are offered by organisations such as the Antwerp Police College which, in 1989, offered policemen and police officers in training a new three-week course on dealing with hazardous wastes. The Fire School of the National Association for Fire Prevention (ANPI) offers training in fire prevention which can be geared to the requirements of individual public or private establishments. It has already been asked for help by several firms faced with the management of hazardous wastes.

Although controlling pollution is part of several degree and other higher education courses offered by universities, the scope is limited, and the UWE are shortly to start environmental training courses at the Business School for Advanced Training in Management (EPM). These will include the management of wastes.

Driver training courses on the Transportation of Dangerous Goods by Road (ADR) are offered by a number of approved organisations, all of whom are required to charge a registration fee that will cover expenses only. In the field of shipping, Depauw and Stokoe, in the port of Antwerp, offer courses for ships' personnel in the handling of hazardous products, and the naval school includes courses on chemical products in its basic training for seafarers. None of this training relates specifically to hazardous wastes.

1.5.2 Denmark

Various organisations in Denmark offer courses that are relevant, at least in part, to those involved in the handling and management of hazardous wastes. Perhaps the most important training is that organised by the Ministry of Labour for the private labour market. This includes the Labour Market Training System (the AMU system) which offers a number of courses related to hazardous substances and to a more limited extent hazardous wastes. The Association of Danish Employers and the Federation of Danish Trade Unions offer environmental and safety courses. The Association of Danish Engineers regularly offers courses on oil and chemical wastes and on contaminated industrial sites. These courses are aimed at engineers and technicians in private companies and the public sector. The Technological Institute runs a number of higher-level courses on reception arrangements for oil and chemical wastes and oil and chemical-contaminated soils.

Kommunkemi, as well as training its own staff, offers courses to other companies and organisations, for example employees at transfer stations and reception depots for waste. In addition, the private company, The Dangerous Goods Consultancy, which does most of its training in connection with transport, includes some consideration of wastes, while a number of other companies run their own internal training courses.

1.5.3 France

In France, a number of bodies and institutions are involved in safety training. The National Institute for Research and Safety (INRS), for instance, not only produces information such as toxicological information sheets, but also provides training programmes for agents of government bodies responsible for monitoring, and for personnel in insurance organisations etc.

Safety training in the transportation of dangerous products is provided by the Association for Vocational Training relating to Transportation (AFT) and by the Association for Accident Prevention in the Transportation of Hydrocarbons (APTH), but neither of these organisations includes specific instruction on wastes.

However, the National Agency for the Recovery and Disposal of Wastes (ANRED) and the Water-Basin Authorities do disseminate information on wastes, publish relevant literature and organise conferences. Several other organisations offer occasional courses relating to hazardous wastes, and of particular importance is the National Institute of Applied Sciences at Lyons.

1.5.4 Germany

The German education system aims to incorporate some environmental education at all levels. In addition, an extensive range of specialist advanced courses has been established for waste producers, waste transporters, waste handlers and disposers, and reclaimers of contaminated land. For example, in North Rhine-Westphalia, training is provided leading to the status of 'waste technician'. Training to 'environment assistant' is also available as is a postgraduate level course leading to qualification as 'waste consultant/waste-management consultant'. There is also vocational training for 'suppliers and disposers'. This is skilled worker training, and subsequent additional training can lead to 'supervisor' status.

1.5.5 Greece

Greece offers no specific courses in the handling and management of hazardous wastes.

1.5.6 Ireland

In Ireland, training is predominantly on the job. Driver safety training courses, the HAZCHEM courses, are now run by a commercial company, and EOLAS, the Irish Science and Technology Agency offers regular courses on biological effluent treatment, activated sludge plant and chemical hazards. Most other courses are run on an occasional basis by companies specialising in the handling of toxic and dangerous waste, and the standard of much of the training is at a rudimentary level.

1.5.7 Italy

An extensive range of courses are available in Italy (However, there is little information about who runs these courses or who attends them).

1.5.8 Luxembourg

Apart from some rudimentary training in the subject for the Fire Service, Luxembourg undertakes no specific training in the area of toxic and dangerous wastes and there is little training on general environmental issues. Occasional lectures and symposia are organised, but most training takes place abroad. Driver training (for the ADR certificate) is organised by the Chamber of Commerce in Luxembourg City.

1.5.9 Netherlands

The Netherlands offers a number of courses specifically related to hazardous wastes. The Dutch Institute for Working Conditions, for instance, includes courses on Healthy and Safe Working with Contaminated Land, on Handling Hazardous Materials, and on Health and Safety in Chemical and Medical Laboratories. Health, safety and welfare courses are also provided by the Institute for Employee Participation, while some Consultancy Bureaus work within industry and help companies to put together training programmes which are relevant to their specific hazard situations.

The General Shippers and Private Transport Organisation (EVO) provides training including that related to the transportation of dangerous goods on the highway, and working within the EC Agreement.

A course for the small chemical waste disposal manager has been set up by the Dutch Association of Sanitary Superintendents (NVRD). This deals with risks to health, the dangers of fire and explosion and the risks connected with the mixing of materials.

1.5.10 Portugal

The Portuguese educational system pays a limited amount of attention to matters of health and safety at primary and secondary levels. Several organisations, notably the Directorate-General for Health and Safety at Work (DGHST) and the Insurance Training Centre (CEFOS) run a number of courses on health and safety at work, but there is no specific training in relation to hazardous wastes.

1.5.11 Spain

In Spain, money has recently been made available under the National Toxic and Dangerous Wastes Plan for promotion, information and publicity campaigns, but public administrations still have no practical training programme as regards wastes. Furthermore, although the Ministry of Public Works and Town and Country Planning (MOPU) organises occasional seminars on environment-related topics, none of the various bodies and institutions dealing with health and safety or the environment have any course or training programme on wastes.

Most of the training in Spain on health and safety, on labour regulations, on the transportation of dangerous goods etc. is offered by private enterprises, often insurance companies. In addition, companies run courses for their own personnel. These courses are usually designed to publicise and explain new legislation and are usually for higher and intermediate technical personnel.

1.5.12 UK

A number of useful courses exist in the UK. Loughborough University, for instance, runs both an introductory and an advanced course in hazardous waste management and introduced, in 1989, a Hazardous Waste Diploma Course. This Diploma provides, for the first time an academic qualification at postgraduate level, dedicated to hazardous waste management and validated by a UK university. The course is designed for industrial managers, waste disposal and treatment contractors, regulatory officers and engineering and environmental consultants.

The Institute of Waste Management Diploma in Waste Management is offered by a number of colleges throughout the UK, and the Institute is also proposing to introduce a Certificate of Competence to increase levels of professionalism in wastes management and to improve standards of training and competence. The National Association of Waste Disposal Contractors run a variety of courses throughout the year. These are highly regarded but are not designed specifically for the handling and management of hazardous wastes. A distance learning course on hazardous waste is also available together with standard driver training courses.

2.0 EDUCATION AND TRAINING OF PERSONNEL WORKING AT HAZARDOUS WASTE FACILITIES

2.1 Background of Personnel Involved in the Handling and Treatment of Hazardous Wastes

2.1.1 General

Very few regulations exist within the 12 Member States of the EC concerning the background and qualifications required by those involved in the handling and treatment of hazardous wastes. Specific reference is made to an Italian regulation which stipulates that only those who have obtained a junior diploma by examination are permitted to handle toxic chemicals. In several countries, however, regulations do stipulate that those responsible for the management, handling and treatment of hazardous wastes must be properly qualified.

In Belgium, the relevant regulations concern only managers or responsible persons. Under the Law of 22 July, 1974 and the Walloon Regional Executive Order of 12 November, 1987, it is compulsory to place any operation involving the disposal of toxic or dangerous wastes under the authority of a responsible chemist who must have adequate experience in this field. Under the Regional Orders on controlled landfills (Flemish Executive Order of 21 April, 1982 and Walloon Regional Executive Order of 23 July, 1987) it is compulsory for acceptance and unloading/decanting operations to be carried out under the supervision and in the presence of the operator or his representative. In the Walloon region, a responsible chemist is expressly responsible for the day-to-day supervision of operating conditions. In practice, managers and responsible persons are university graduates or possess university-type higher education diplomas (A1 diplomas). They are generally chemists or specialist engineers.

The standard of education of operational personnel in Belgium varies between the lowest (primary) level of education and the A1 diploma level. In general, the standard of education of unskilled workers is very low (primary level) while skilled workers usually possess higher secondary education certificates in chemistry or technical subjects.

In France, where nearly all the treatment centres for dangerous industrial wastes and landfill sites for special industrial wastes are run by large enterprises or by subsidiaries of large industrial groups, the average level of education and technical skill is rising. On average, 50% of personnel have basic school education; 20% have some additional vocational training, and 30% have secondary or higher education.

In the Netherlands, a survey of companies involved in the handling or processing of chemical wastes was undertaken. This revealed that the majority of personnel working for the companies contacted had completed their formal education between the ages of 16 and 19 years.

The majority of the companies surveyed indicated that training was sufficiently thorough for working with hazardous wastes. Nevertheless, a need for further training was expressed by a significant number of correspondents, especially in the areas of materials identification, safe working procedures involving chemical waste, and the legislation relating to these materials.

Hazardous waste management in Spain is still in the early stages of development. The Regulations on Toxic and Dangerous Wastes make certain stipulations, namely:

- that plant directors must have higher education qualifications;

- that the person in charge of laboratories must be a specialist with higher education qualifications;

- that those in charge of operation and maintenance must be technical personnel with qualifications at least to secondary education level;

- that other personnel must have the qualifications and training appropriate to the functions they perform.

(Because the response to the survey was so limited, there is little factual detail about actual qualifications.)

2.1.2 Plants Storing and Treating Their Own Wastes

In most Member States where industrial concerns store and treat their own hazardous wastes, the educational levels encountered among management are high. In Denmark, for instance, managers are typically engineers, while technical and skilled personnel have undergone some form of vocational training. In Portugal academic qualifications at graduate or diploma level are usual for technical managers, while middle management staff have normally completed either the standard general educational course (nine years of schooling) or the additional course (11-12 years of schooling). Those who have completed the latter have usually studied technical subjects.

In Ireland, the supervisory staff responsible for hazardous waste storage and treatment will be mainly chemical engineers or chemists educated to graduate (and occasionally postgraduate) level, the only exceptions being where the levels of toxicity and the quantities produced are minimal. Furthermore, the same staff will normally have received prior training in the handling of such waste, either at a parent company abroad or at the commissioning stage on site. The extent of this training depends both on the size of the company and on the extent of waste treatment required.

At the operative level, standards of education are normally much lower. In most countries, unskilled workers have not usually received any prior training in the handling of hazardous wastes and have normally only completed their basic education. This, however, varies in length. In Portugal, for instance, although the younger workers have generally completed the nine-year standard general course, some of the older operatives have perhaps only six years' schooling (primary level) and the survey revealed that in one pesticides firm the personnel operating the incineration and effluent treatment plant had received only four years' schooling.

German chemical and pharmaceutical companies, particularly the larger concerns, have established high standards. Between 60 and 80% of the staff employed by the large chemical companies are trained personnel, and in certain very sensitive areas, the percentage may rise to 100%. However disposal matters do not form a regular component even of university training courses for chemists and chemical engineers, nor are wastes always properly disposed of at these establishments, so firms cannot assume that even their highly qualified staff have appropriate levels of awareness and knowledge concerning wastes.

2.1.3 Independent Treatment Plants and Transfer Stations

The overall lack of any minimum educational or training requirement is equally true for independent treatment plants and transfer stations. Throughout the EC, the tendency is for managers/

supervisors to be educated to degree or postgraduate level, usually in engineering or chemistry, or to be skilled machine operators. Technical staff are generally trained electricians, mechanics etc., as appropriate, while most operatives have received little more than the basic state education.

In West Germany, many of the Federal Provinces now allow companies governed by public law to carry out the disposal of special wastes, and it is assumed that the Technical Directive on Waste, when issued, will include recommendations as to the qualifications of personnel working in the various types of plant concerned. The laboratories involved in waste identification employ specialist personnel almost exclusively. Within the waste treatment companies, many graduates, often with chemistry and chemical engineering specialisms, are employed as technical works managers, particularly in the larger companies. In smaller concerns, fewer managers have either chemistry or high-level academic qualifications. This does not necessarily pose a major problem because the nature of the work determines that most relevant knowledge is acquired at work rather than by attendance at courses. Operatives usually have no relevant formal qualifications.

In Luxembourg, only one company, the Société Lamesch, includes the management of toxic and dangerous wastes among its activities. Approximately 10% of the workforce is employed in the toxic waste area, working under a technical director, a technical engineer (with qualifications a little above the baccalaureat level) and six chemists, most of whom have gained the A2 diploma. Drivers and handlers are unskilled and generally of a very low level of educational achievement. Drivers are therefore employed on a four-month trial period, while handlers are normally recruited from existing company employees in whom the management has confidence.

In general terms, the level of educational qualification/training required by those working in independent treatment plants and transfer stations will to some extent depend on the level of technical complexity of the facility under consideration.

The safe operation of incinerators for chemical waste, for instance, requires a high level of technical competence and co-ordinated management. Where such plants accept large quantities of highly toxic and polluting waste, a high degree of professionalism is necessary at every stage of the work from unloading to final incineration, and strict operating procedures must be observed. In the UK, operational managers and supervisors are usually qualified to degree level in chemistry, chemical engineering or mechanical engineering. Some also have postgraduate qualifications. Furthermore, most of the senior engineering, laboratory and monitoring staff are also qualified to degree level, and are frequently recruited from the chemical industry, the source of most of the waste. At the operational level, many of the maintenance staff and equipment operators will either have attended day-release courses or served apprenticeships, while those engaged in store keeping, cleaning and basic administration are likely to have received only a general school education.

A similar situation obtains in physical/chemical treatment plants. Again in the UK, most senior technical and supervisory staff are qualified chemists or chemical engineers, and many of them will have attended a hazardous waste management training course of some kind. Equipment operators, maintenance staff and drivers will have the basic state education, although some will be skilled workers and tradesmen.

2.1.4 Landfill Sites

The methods and standards of landfilling hazardous waste vary considerably throughout the Community, however, not withstanding this variation it is still evident that the need for competence in both management and operation is essential if the environment and worker safety are to be safeguarded. Every aspect of landfill operation must be subject to adequate procedures, particularly:

- the monitoring and inspection of incoming waste;
- the careful management of the tipping face and of waste compaction;
- containment and control of leachate;
- borehole monitoring;
- methane management.

This requires personnel not only to have adequate scientific, analytical and engineering skills, but also for all personnel to be properly managed.

In the UK for instance, where 79% of hazardous wastes are disposed of at co-disposal sites, poor regulation of sites has resulted in numerous instances of illegal disposal and local environmental contamination. The structure of the industry is such that there are many small, independent and local-authority run sites as well as a small number of large waste disposal companies running large disposal facilities. Recent improvements have taken place at some sites, particularly in waste acceptance and handling procedures, and some site laboratories staffed by qualified chemists have been set up. All sites must be licensed under the Control of Pollution Act, 1974, but the licences do not stipulate the educational/training requirements for personnel and most supervisors have received only basic school education.

A typical situation in Greece, where 90% of all hazardous waste disposals are by landfill, is for a site foreman to be responsible for between six and eight unskilled operatives. The supervisor will not be educated to diploma or degree level, and the operatives require no specific qualifications.

In France, the rising educational levels of newly recruited personnel employed in hazardous waste disposal facilities are reflected in the figures for landfill operations. Seventy percent of employees in the major company, which operates seven of the 11 landfill sites for hazardous waste, have basic education or basic education plus vocational skills; 13% have secondary level education and 17% have undergone higher education.

2.2 Existing Training Provision

2.2.1 General

Very little legislation has been passed by Member States in respect of the training of personnel involved in the handling and monitoring of hazardous wastes. Most countries rely on existing legislation concerning safety at work to protect the interests of employees. As a result, actual training in the handling and monitoring of hazardous wastes varies considerably from one State to another.

In Belgium, the Règlement Général pour la Protection du Travail (RGPT) sets out the basic statutory provisions on safety at work, including the waste sector. These include appropriate training for the work, and the provision of information regarding hazardous substances, the likely degree of danger, the conditions for the use of certain substances and fire measures. Supplementary training is stipulated for heads of safety and their deputies.

As regards hazardous waste in particular, most training is undertaken within the firm, usually through supervision by managers. This method allows updating to take place and helps to make up for the fact that workers lack both knowledge and an awareness of risks. Because direct communication is involved, together with supervision, such training is regarded as effective.

Some firms supplement this type of training with more structured in-house or external training on topics such as safety, the handling of chemical products and risks. Training in larger firms is generally more structured, and technical training may be provided by the Head Office of a large company.

At the management level, there is a high level of participation by directors and managers in seminars or conferences relating directly or indirectly to the problem of waste. Such events provide a forum for the comparison of problems or for the establishment of business relationships, and may sometimes involve travel abroad - to Germany, the Netherlands, USA or Denmark.

Only one course, that organised by the Centre for Study and Research on Safety, Ergonomics and the Promotion of Working Conditions (CRESEPT), provides specific training on the management of hazardous wastes. It is aimed at those who are usually already highly qualified - safety managers, works medical officers, chemists and engineers.

In France, there is a high degree of interest in safety and training, even though, in some organisations such training has only recently been introduced. Training is designed for the job, and all personnel have the opportunity to attend training courses which, nowadays, are run with the help of outside training bodies. These courses may take place either in-house or externally. Teaching methods include the use of lectures, videos and on-site practical work.

In general, the training is facilitated by the concentration of hazardous waste treatment and monitoring in the hands of a small number of organisations. Training appears to be correctly targeted and motivation is good. In fact those facing the highest risks, for instance at cement works treating and using organic industrial wastes as fuel, are usually the most demanding as regards training. Because of the specific nature of each course, there is sometimes difficulty in finding appropriate outside help for particular aspects of training. Most external training facilities are therefore oriented to special topics such as wastes chemistry, practical firefighting and first aid.

The situation in Italy is in stark contrast to that in France. In Italy the structure of the waste disposal industry, with a large number of scattered units each employing only a small number of technical personnel, poses practical difficulties in terms of training. Because of limited manpower, most firms cannot release staff for training without shutting down the plant. Furthermore, fierce competition limits the opportunities for shared training programmes, and the high cost of courses organised by private bodies is an additional deterrent. As a result, job training is not formalised and consists of on-the-job training while new recruits are being familiarised with their work. Those general courses which are available to industrial concerns are designed to inform technical and administrative staff about regulations and correct procedures. They are not designed for workers dealing directly with hazardous waste products.

The provision of training in hazardous waste management in Spain is very poor or non-existent. Most waste management enterprises use their own technical personnel to provide such training. Most of the training material is taken from technical journals, specialist books etc. and is hard to come by. Any external courses and seminars are usually of a very general nature. It is, however, anticipated that, with the establishment of the National Toxic and Dangerous Wastes Plan, training programmes will be developed in the near future.

2.2.2 Plants Storing and Treating Their Own Waste

About half of the chemical waste produced in the Netherlands is treated by the companies themselves. Some of these companies are authorised to treat waste from other companies as well as their own. Most of the companies involved provide their own specific training, and the Dutch Chemical Association has an important role to play in providing appropriate education and training for its members.

In Denmark, the survey identified a considerable variation in training facilities. Some firms have no special training in this area of work, while others have developed their own internal courses, sometimes establishing their own separate training department or a safety department which is responsible for training. Some external training is also available, for instance at the Technological Institute, at AMU (Labour Market Training system) centres and at craft trade colleges.

Probably because of the high level of trained personnel employed by the larger German companies in particular, personnel at the operational level are largely trained on the job. New work safety and environmental protection elements are being introduced into training programmes, and attention is being given to remedying the current deficiency in teaching and learning materials and trainer training.

There is a distinct lack of relevant courses in Ireland, even for middle management and supervisors. The Federation of the Irish Chemical Industry (the relevant trade association) has no systematic involvement in training although it does organise occasional courses on topics of general interest. General safety training (not specifically on toxic or hazardous waste aspects) for unskilled workers is followed by on-the-job training in the area of work assigned. The survey noted that workers complained about the lack of formal training in the hazards associated with their work, a particular concern being that other staff might not follow the required procedures. Some companies are now considering setting up internal training courses using their own plus external staff.

Although the number of workers involved is small, training conditions in Portugal vary considerably from one firm to another. Those firms responding to the survey all provided the necessary safety training required by law. In one plant manufacturing isocyanates, all workers complete a general two-day safety course when they join, and subsequently attend monthly safety sessions. Although most of those involved with hazardous waste are subcontractors, the same safety conditions apply to them as to the firm's full-time employees. In another firm manufacturing integrated circuits, employees do not start work until they have received the relevant safety training and information on in-house safety regulations. However, the training at most firms is related to all aspects of work and not specifically to hazardous wastes.

2.2.3 Independent treatment plants and transfer stations

The position on training in the independent treatment plants can best be shown by a number of case studies. All companies dealing with hazardous wastes provide the necessary instruction/training to ensure the safety of their employees and to comply with the relevant safety at work regulations. Inevitably, the scope of that training will depend on the degree of hazard involved.

At one incineration plant for chemical waste in the Netherlands, for instance, there is an introductory programme for new employees detailing the nature of the work, the associated dangers and the preventive measures to be taken. Safety regulations exist; there is an emergency plan for disasters, and all employees are given instructions about how to react to alarms. Additional instructional programmes have also been devised for employees on safety and health in connection with their work. Examples include a course on the safe handling of chlorine and another on safety equipment. The safety motivation plan includes a course for management on the carrying out of inspections, and associated reporting.

Similar procedures are characteristic of a thermal cleaning plant for contaminated soil. On joining the company, and every subsequent year, employees are informed by a safety expert on the nature of the work, its associated dangers and the preventive measures to be taken. Employees are also regularly informed, both verbally and in writing, of the purpose, effect and use of safety equipment, and how to act in dangerous situations. Participation in such instruction is mandatory. There are also a number of external training courses in specific work areas for employees, although there are no such information/instruction programmes for management. Two external expert services are associated with the company, one dealing with industrial health and the other a private safety consultant.

Mandatory courses are also part of the training involved at a physical/chemical cleaning plant in the Netherlands. This company collects and physically separates chemical wastes and undertakes the emptying and cleaning of industrial tanks on site. Apart from internal regulations on escape routes, first aid, bans on smoking, the packing and identification of wastes, and the availability and use of both fire-fighting and personal safety equipment, new employees are informed by the works manager of the dangers associated with the work and on preventive measures to be taken. In addition, certain external training courses are mandatory, notably on the transportation of dangerous substances, and a practical safety course given by the Factory Inspectorate.

In the UK, companies operating physical/chemical treatment plants have generally accumulated a great deal of expertise. Most training is therefore internal and undertaken by management and supervisory staff in the course of the work. Although some senior technical and supervisory staff may attend externally organised training courses in hazardous waste management and other more general waste management seminars and short courses on legislative changes, safety procedures, etc.

Training is facilitated in Denmark by the concentration of much of the country's hazardous waste treatment at KOMMUNEKEMI. Not only does KOMMUNEKEMI run regular training courses for its own personnel, but it offers courses to other companies, for instance transfer stations and reception depots handling oil and chemical wastes: these courses are well attended and are regarded as excellent. KOMMUNEKEMI provides regular training for its personnel at all levels. Each winter there is a nine-day course for white collar workers which includes personnel management and safety. The training staff for this course include employees from KOMMUNEKEMI's own Vocational and Training Department, together with some external tutors. This course is often held off-site at the Great Belt Centre.

On-site courses include monthly introductory courses for new employees, an annual five-day introductory course for those in their first year of appointment, and annual refresher courses for both skilled and semi-skilled workers on safety problems and fire drill. The five-day course is likely to include technology, safety, and training in the handling of oil and chemical wastes. Staff from the Vocational Training Department, managers from the incineration division, maintenance managers and others act as trainers.

Most other hazardous waste treatment companies also give priority to training. Sometimes this training is provided by external courses run by the Technological Institute (TI), the AMU or local craft trades colleges. Where, however, such courses do not meet specific requirements, internal training has been established, for both skilled and unskilled workers. Refresher courses are also regarded as important.

A similar concentration of training activities occurs in Luxembourg where the Société Lamesch is the only plant concerned with the collection, sorting, transportation and, to a certain extent, treatment of toxic and dangerous wastes. Employers are obliged to instruct their employees when they start work and once each year thereafter on the dangers specific to their activities and on how to minimise them. Work with hazardous wastes may only be entrusted to those who are competent and duly informed of the dangers. Fire training and driver training are undertaken within Luxembourg, but most other external training is undertaken in Germany and elsewhere. All drivers and handlers, for instance, attend a three to four day refresher course in Germany on chemical problems. Some members of the commercial department and some chemists have attended courses abroad on the taking of samples, and senior staff regularly attend seminars abroad, again especially in Germany.

Elsewhere, the situation varies. In Ireland, for instance, most hazardous waste contractors operate as middlemen, frequently hiring bulk tankers to transport waste from the producer to the UK. Most of these firms are small, owner-managed operations, in competition with one another. There appears to be little structured training, even in the handling of asbestos waste, and the lack of formal training courses for workers and management in the handling of asbestos waste is a source of some concern.

In the UK, all new employees at incinerator plants for toxic waste receive some formal in-house training by senior employees: this covers safety, emergency procedures, site management and organisation and will last for periods varying from one day to several weeks depending on the responsibilities and duties of the employee. All new employees also receive training specific to their job responsibilities and duties. Because few of these plants exist, there is little demand for externally organised training, and most of the companies involved have considerable in-house expertise. Nevertheless, some senior managers and supervisors are required or encouraged to attend relevant courses and seminars.

The situation in Germany is far less structured than one might expect. Training appears to be regarded by all staff as important, yet, in spite of the wide range of advanced level courses available, many companies do not appear to have well structured training policies. Management training, for instance, is not always of much relevance to the handling and management of hazardous wastes. Some of the larger companies however, in co-operation with an individual training establishment, have drafted plans for training courses for their middle management and laboratory staff which are tailor-made for their requirements. This level of commitment and preparation is often beyond the scope of smaller companies, particularly because of the problems of staff replacement during training. Operational staff are trained on a regular basis to meet statutory safety requirements. However, systematic training, or training outside the company, is the absolute exception.

2.2.4 Landfill Sites

Apart from France, where the structure of the hazardous waste disposal industry differs in scale from most other countries, there is little formal training for either supervisors or manual workers on landfill sites. Even in France, the safety training is less comprehensive than in other sectors of the hazardous waste handling and treatment industry, mainly because the waste handled is not usually truly hazardous waste. However, those dealing with the reception of waste (where most problems are likely to arise) appear to be adequately trained.

In the UK few on-site landfill supervisors are likely to have received any formal training from their employer in waste management. Nor are they likely to have attended any externally organised short courses and seminars on hazardous waste management. In Greece, too, most supervisors receive only on-the-job training, possibly while acting as assistant to a supervisor. Most operatives are similarly trained on an informal basis on site although, in Greece, they may occasionally attend one-day seminars. These are arranged by site operators and cover such topics as safety and hygiene issues, theoretical methods of safe landfill and dealing with or avoiding contact with leachates. No statutory training courses are provided in either country.

2.3 Gaps and Needs in the Existing Training Provision

The Danish study identified a need for good external courses on chemical wastes, and for refresher courses. In Germany, substantial gaps in knowledge of waste disposal technology were identified for plants other than chemical plants.

Both Belgian and French surveys identified a need for refresher courses. Apart from the management seminars mentioned above, no refresher courses are available in Belgium. In France, however, most organisations do run such courses, although these appear to vary in both quality and frequency.

In the UK, at landfill sites, as there are no agreed criteria for judging the adequacy and experience of those employed, it is difficult to stipulate what training courses are needed. In Ireland, the lack of formal training for workers and management in the handling of asbestos was seen as a major gap.

In Germany, third party disposers operating on a small scale often cannot manage the commitment and preparation needed for middle-management and laboratory staff training. Furthermore, in some of the smaller firms, some of the statutory regulations are not even observed, mainly through ignorance. There is a major training opportunity here as the range of training is inadequate.

The Italian survey noted that it would be desirable to insist on a minimum educational level in the waste disposal sector: school education should extend over the lower secondary cycle, with job prospects in this sector based on an examination to assess the minimum educational background. Staff should also be made fully aware of the risks for themselves, their colleagues and the environment.

Training in Spain in the area of hazardous wastes handling and management is entirely inadequate in general terms. An entire training programme needs to be set up and implemented.

2.4 Conclusions and Recommendations

2.4.1 Conclusions

- Member States have passed very little legislation concerning the background and educational level required of those involved in the handling and treatment of hazardous wastes. The main requirements for most countries are that managers and responsible persons must be appropriately qualified, although specific qualifications are not normally stipulated.

- In practice, the educational level of management and supervisory personnel is high. Managers are typically educated to at least degree and diploma level, usually in chemistry or chemical engineering. To some extent, however, the level of qualification demanded will depend on the level of technical complexity of the facility under consideration. Chemical waste incineration plants demand high level qualifications of their management and supervisory staff, while landfill sites in several countries are often supervised by staff with little more than basic school education plus some relevant work experience.

- Most operatives have completed little more than basic schooling, and have not received any prior training in the handling of hazardous wastes. Furthermore, the length of schooling varies to some extent from country to country. Some of the workers in one Portuguese plant were found to have completed only four years of schooling. In the more sophisticated plants, operatives may have attended day-release courses or completed apprenticeships.

- There is little statutory provision for training in the handling and management of hazardous wastes. Most countries rely on existing health and safety legislation to protect the interests of employees.

- Actual training provision varies from one Member State to another. A high proportion of training, particularly in the area of health and safety at work is undertaken in-house by the companies concerned. Opportunities for operative training externally are the exception rather than the rule, although management and supervisory staff are encouraged to take advantage of seminars and conferences on relevant topics where these are available. To some extent training reflects the structure of the industry. Where hazardous waste facilities are small-scale and widely scattered, small staff numbers and the cost of training restricts both the development of internal and attendance at external courses. In countries such as France, where hazardous waste treatment is concentrated in the hands of a small number of large organisations, training can be more effectively organised.

- It is recognised that there is a continual turnover of employees at many waste treatment, disposal and transfer facilities, i.e. the workforce is not stable, and therefore, company managers are often reluctant to provide expensive training.

- The number of relevant external training courses is limited. In general, those countries with a longer experience of handling hazardous wastes can offer a greater number and variety of relevant courses.

- A major gap identified in various countries was the need for appropriate refresher courses.

- There would appear to be major opportunities for the development of training in countries such as Spain and Greece where training provision is virtually non-existent, and also in other countries where the structure of the industry or of sections of the industry hinders the development of training schemes.

2.4.2 Recommendations

The following paragraphs summarise the specific recommendations made by individual countries.

- There should be some degree of standardisation of qualification requirements for special waste disposal facilities.

- Every firm should appoint an officer with specific responsibility for the environment.

- Countries lacking any basic training facilities should establish a basic training programme and possibly a training centre.

- All courses in environmental sciences and techniques, wherever located, should consider the question of hazardous wastes in greater detail.

- Every firm should develop appropriate training programmes.

- More courses (with practical demonstrations) on properties of chemicals and their toxicity should be developed.

- There should be more training in the operation of incinerators and other specialised waste facilities.

- There should be more professional qualifications in waste management particularly in the landfill sector and for certain other workers, e.g. incinerator operators.

3.0 EDUCATION AND TRAINING OF PERSONNEL INVOLVED IN THE TRANSPORTATION OF HAZARDOUS WASTES

3.1 Road Transport

3.1.1 Importance of Road Transport in the Transportation of Hazardous Wastes

Although there is some slight variation between Member States in the proportion of hazardous wastes carried by road, this form of transport is the one most frequently used for the transportation of such substances. In France, the UK, Italy and Greece for instance, road transport is the main means of transporting hazardous waste. Rail transport features to a limited extent in Denmark, West Germany, Belgium and, to some extent Spain, while inland navigation features significantly only in those countries with well established and well-used canal systems, namely the Netherlands, West Germany and Belgium. Sea transport is of greater significance to countries such as Netherlands and Belgium, with their major international ports, Denmark (because of its geography), and Ireland (where a large proportion of the hazardous waste produced is exported for treatment).

3.1.2 Background of Personnel Involved

There is no specific legislation in Member States concerning the standard of education of those involved in the transportation of hazardous waste by road and most drivers employed have a very low standard of education. In Belgium, for instance, a typical driver background comprises a primary or lower secondary vocational level of education. In France, the background is usually basic school plus vocational training, although most recruitment is from among the ranks of experienced lorry drivers.

However, there are regulations concerning levels of initial training for certain types of road transport. In Belgium and Luxembourg, a training certificate, in accordance with the European Agreement Concerning the International Carriage of Dangerous Goods by Road (ADR), is compulsory for drivers carrying hazardous substances in tanker bodies, tanks or multiple tanks with a total capacity of 3,000 litres or more, although there are certain exemptions. Since 1st January 1988, in the Netherlands, all drivers engaged in either national or international transportation of dangerous substances in the same types of container must be in possession of the same certificate or of a CCV certificate for the Transportation of Dangerous Goods by Road. Frequently drivers are required to have these certificates before they are employed. However, it should be noted that ADR training deals only with pure products, and incorporates only a few theoretical considerations on rules forbidding combined loads. Most hazardous wastes involve combinations of products.

The UK has a similar statutory training requirement for tanker drivers (extended in April 1988 to cover any vehicle carrying dangerous substances), as does Denmark. In the UK, many drivers undertake this training prior to applying for a job as the certificate is frequently a prerequisite to employment.

In Germany, the 'Law relating to the transport of hazardous goods' and the 'Decree relating to the internal and trans-frontier transport of hazardous goods by road (Hazardous Goods Decree, Road Transport)' derived from it, requires that only trained drivers may be entrusted with the transportation of hazardous materials. In Ireland, drivers transporting any dangerous substance must receive training under the Dangerous Substances (Conveyance of Scheduled Substances by Road) (Trade or Business) Regulations of 1980. Apart from asbestos waste, which is likely to be included under new legislation, the transportation by road of all toxic and dangerous wastes is regarded as coming under this law.

In Portugal, drivers of vehicles transporting dangerous goods must have a certificate verifying that they have successfully completed a training course relating to the specific safety requirements of the job. In Spain too, special courses are a legal requirement laid down by the Regulations on the Transportation of Dangerous Goods by Road.

It must, however, be emphasised that, in all cases where regulations are laid down concerning the qualifications of drivers transporting hazardous substances, the regulations nearly always refer to pure substances rather than to hazardous wastes. In Denmark, the obligatory special training for drivers transporting mixed cargoes of dangerous goods was considered and rejected. In the Netherlands, proper qualifications for the mixed transportation of dangerous goods are likely to be enforced in 1996, perhaps even earlier.

At the management level, backgrounds vary. In Belgium, managers of large and medium sized firms involved in this type of transport are usually graduate engineers or chemists or holders of A1 diplomas in these subjects. In France too, the larger enterprises are now recruiting technical personnel with higher educational levels, while in Spain management personnel usually have higher or secondary qualifications, while supervisors and foremen have usually completed intermediate level vocational training.

3.1.3 Existing Training Provision

All employers must comply with national legislation concerning safety at work, and this applies as much in the transport sector as in any other area of work. Because most of the existing legislation concerning training provision for those involved in transportation relates to hazardous substances in general and not hazardous wastes in particular, the training is also of a more general nature, with some reference to specific pure substances.

Most of the training provided is for drivers.

ADR training, as stated above, is only for pure products, as are the ADR safety cards, and there are no drills or practical exercises on mixtures of products. The training comprises:

- the basic course covering topics relating to all hazardous substances;
- at least one of four specialist courses relating to particular categories of dangerous goods:
- gases
- solids and liquids except those below
- ammonium nitrate
- radioactive materials

The training covers statutory regulations, road conduct, classification of hazardous substances, documentation, special markings and emergency measures. The certificate issued is valid for five years and must then be renewed either after a refresher course, or after provision of proof of uninterrupted employment in the specialisms for which the original certificate was granted. Further renewals are required at five-year intervals up to the age of 65. Between 65 and 70 annual renewal must be accompanied by a medical certificate.

In Belgium, the ADR certificate is issued by the Transport Authority of the Ministry of Communications. Training may take place either externally or within companies: it lasts for about 5 days and includes practical exercises. In Luxembourg, the training takes place under the auspices of the Chamber of Commerce, and the certificate is awarded by the Minister for Transport after a course of at least 24 hours of instruction and including a final examination.

In Belgium, ADR training in relation to the transportation of hazardous wastes has been supplemented by additional in-house training. Often, however, this consists simply of supervision by responsible persons to allow the necessary updating to be done. Some firms organise courses and provide videos for viewing and discussion by multi-skilled operatives. The only external course available is that run by CRESEPT (see above, Section 2.2). This does include a transport component but is designed for those who are already highly qualified in hazardous waste management.

In Luxembourg, the Société Lamesch requires all vehicles to carry safety instructions in case of accident. These are provided by the supplier of the substances concerned and include (in the language of the Member States concerned) details of the hazard and the safety measures to be taken, and details of measures to be taken if packaging deteriorates or a spillage occurs. These safety cards, however, are inadequate for the transportation of hazardous waste as they apply only to pure products.

In the Netherlands, the course 'Transportation of Dangerous Goods on the Highway (ADR)' is a response to the minimum standard qualifications which have been imposed. The course pays special attention to chemical waste throughout and is designed for tanker drivers and others likely to be concerned - the police, fire services etc. A final examination is involved.

Driver training in the transportation of dangerous substances, including practical training, is also provided as part of the apprentice system, and a ten-day course for national tank transporters is offered by the Institute of Professional Road Transport Training at its Lunteren study centre. The same organisation is also developing a course specifically geared to the transportation of chemical waste.

Some road transport companies supplement the general training courses available, by providing specific in-house practical training. New driver training courses are being organised in collaboration with some major manufacturers and forwarders.

Other Member States have similar patterns of training. In Germany, ADR training, which has to be updated by a one-day course every five years, involves a basic course for all hazard classes together with various compulsory training courses for the following classes of substance:

- compressed, liquefied or pressurised-solute gases
- inflammable liquids
- ignitable substances
- toxic substances
- corrosive substances.

In France, statutory requirements for the transportation of dangerous goods in general are covered by training which is attended by all operating personnel except administrative and commercial staff. The training methods include practical on-the-job exercises and video sessions. End-of-course examinations are held, and refresher courses are compulsory every four years. The result has been a drop in accidents and improved safety procedures. Most training is provided by the Association for Vocational Training relating to Transportation (AFT) and by the Association for the Prevention of Accidents in the Transportation of Hydrocarbons (APTH). In addition, there is a general practice, after an accident, of bringing together the personnel concerned to reduce the likelihood of mistakes being repeated and to improve safety standards. Within companies, it is common for a new recruit to be paired with a particularly experienced and skilled worker who acts as instructor.

In Ireland, three-day HAZCHEM courses are held approximately monthly at various centres throughout the country. They are designed for drivers who transport dangerous substances and are very well attended. Their effectiveness and the professional approach of hauliers is confirmed by the Police, who find that documentation is normally correct.

Some degree of standardisation in statutory driver training has been achieved in the UK. Although the large waste disposal companies have typically introduced their own in-house training courses, a number of independent training organisations exist for drivers from the smaller companies. Tanker driver training courses typically last for three days, and practical training is undertaken by the haulage companies using their own vehicles. The training organisations also provide specific courses for managers, supervisors, vehicle operators, police and fire officers involved in the handling and transportation of hazardous materials. As in most other countries, the training is for hazardous substances in general rather than specifically for hazardous wastes.

There are no courses provided in Denmark which are fully relevant to the transportation of hazardous wastes. The Road Transport College gives training in the transportation of dangerous goods in general, and the Dangerous Goods Consultancy (FGK) also provides training relevant to hazardous wastes. Most training in small companies is, however, on-the-job training.

The new Spanish Regulations on Toxic and Dangerous Wastes means that all movements of hazardous wastes will now be recorded and properly monitored. Up to now there has been little control. A number of hauliers have been licensed to transport certain products in approved vehicles which must undergo regular inspection and, although the survey received very limited response, it concluded that the transport sector is well organised and that personnel are likely to receive the training required by the new regulations. In Portugal, the recent legislation requiring drivers of vehicles transporting dangerous goods to have a certificate verifying that they have successfully completed an appropriate training course has improved the situation. Courses are now structured according to the materials transported, the aim, as elsewhere in the EC, being to make drivers aware of the risks and to provide them with the vital basic knowledge to minimise accidents and their effects. The courses are taught by recognised bodies.

3.1.4 Gaps and Needs in the Existing Training Provision

The gaps and needs in the existing training provision vary considerably from country to country. The main conclusion to be drawn is that, although training regulations exist for the transportation of hazardous substances in general, there is practically no training for hazardous wastes specifically.

In Belgium, the need for more detailed training is recognised but many employers do not give this a high priority. No professional group has yet produced an appropriate training programme and beside this lack of programmes, there is lack of suitably qualified instructors, training equipment, administrative structures and financial resources.

A similar situation obtains in France. The need is recognised for training in the hazardous wastes sector, including a knowledge of the properties of wastes, of their likely behaviour, of the risks involved in mixing wastes, and of the compatibility of products with their containers. Particular problems occur when small quantities of waste are collected from a number of different sources. No policy has been determined by either professionals or authorities, and the fragmentation of this section of the industry compounds the problem. Two changes are, however, likely to improve the situation:

- Agences Financieres de Bassin now offer subsidies to producers of hazardous waste for its transportation and treatment. An approval procedure has been set up whereby collection and transport enterprises are obliged to acquire a certain level of skill.

- Occupational bodies or schemes have been set up, and these represent a positive move towards awakening and promoting a concern for safety in this area.

To date, one course outline has been developed and the APTH is developing special training to counter the risks of pollution in the event of an accident.

In Germany, most of those questioned in the survey suggested that training was both inadequate and too infrequent. The concern of the larger companies that training efforts should be intensified has resulted in a number of compulsory internal courses. However, smaller companies suffering from a considerable degree of competition are unable to afford not only the cost of such training but also the expense of employing drivers with better qualifications.

The situation in Greece is perhaps the least satisfactory one. Because of the lack of legal requirements concerning education and training for drivers or operators of vehicles transporting waste, operational standards depend on the standards implemented by the individual vehicle owner/operator. There are some examples of good practice, especially within the larger industrial complexes, but there is no structured training, and the country suffers from a shortage of qualified personnel, organisations and resources to carry out such training.

3.2 Rail Transport

3.2.1 The Importance of Rail Transport in the Transportation of Hazardous Wastes

Rail transport does not feature significantly in the EC in the transportation of hazardous wastes. For rail transport to be viable, an adequate infrastructure of collection centres and transfer stations must exist. While Spain is planning to build such an infrastructure, including waste treatment plants, over the next five years, few other countries are appropriately positioned in this respect.

3.2.2 Existing training provision

In both Belgium and Luxembourg, international regulations apply to the carriage of dangerous goods by rail plus, in Belgium, the 'tarif 21' which relates specifically to toxic wastes. The chief liability lies with the consignor and neither country offers any specific training in hazardous wastes handling or management for its operatives. Some new training is being introduced in Belgium to allow the international carriage of dangerous goods between the Netherlands, Austria, the Federal Republic of Germany and Belgium without checking at each frontier. Inspection will take place in the country of consignment in each case. The Belgian inspectors will be equipment inspectors with low-level qualifications: their training will not include the handling or management of hazardous wastes.

German regulations involve the 'Decree relating to the internal and trans-frontier transport of hazardous goods by rail (Hazardous Goods Decree, Rail Transport)'. This only indirectly applies minimum qualifications to the personnel carrying out the transportation. For example, verification of the approval for forwarding hazardous goods, by inspection of the documentation, is to be carried out only by personnel familiar with the legal framework concerned and with the actual problems involved, and who are capable of putting this knowledge into practice.

The training itself involves both theoretical and on-the-job instruction, and includes some training content relevant to hazardous goods. Again, as in other countries, no specific training for hazardous wastes is involved.

RENFE, the Spanish railways network, runs courses for its own personnel and for many technical, executive and middle management personnel of enterprises and bodies connected both with transport and with dangerous goods. The courses, which are aimed at middle management, foremen and supervisors, last for three days and concentrate on safety in the transportation of dangerous goods.

3.3 Sea Transport

3.3.1 Importance of Sea Transport in the Transportation of Hazardous Wastes

Only Belgium, Germany, Ireland and the Netherlands responded to the survey in connection with sea transport. Both Belgium and the Netherlands have major European transit ports at Antwerp and Rotterdam respectively, while Ireland relies to a great extent on ferry services for exporting waste for treatment, normally by road tanker.

3.3.2 Background of Personnel Involved

No minimum standards of education are stipulated by law for those involved in the transportation of hazardous wastes by sea. However, the captain of any Belgian vessel has a university-level diploma, and naval schools and colleges provide training up to Officer level in both Belgium and the Netherlands.

3.3.3 Existing Training Provision

Belgian law offers no specific legislation regarding the training of seafarers involved in the transportation of hazardous wastes. However, Belgian law is essentially a transposition of international conventions which include compulsory training for captains, officers, seamen and engineers of tanker vessels carrying chemical products or liquefied gases. Other regulations are in force for those responsible for loading and unloading etc.

The firm Depauw and Stokoe, located in Antwerp Port Zone, gives course to ships' personnel, particularly regarding the handling of dangerous goods and the MARPOL regulations.

In the Netherlands, the naval school and college provide training up to Officer level which includes the transportation of dangerous cargo, regulations, knowledge and use of the dangerous substances manual, and some general chemical knowledge. No specific attention is paid to chemical wastes.

The German 'Decree relating to the carriage of hazardous goods on seagoing vessels (Hazardous Goods Decree, Sea Transport)' specifies safety obligations and procedures to be adopted when handling mixtures and solutions. The producer/supplier has to provide specific data on the substances and their hazard classification, reference sheet numbers for accidents and first-aid procedures. It is also law that reference books must be carried on every Federal German Ship. The load must be constantly supervised, and it is the responsibility of the Master to ensure that the crew are aware of the conditions of transport, of possible risks, and of the procedures to be followed or action to be taken if necessary.

Irish ferry terminal staff would not normally have third-level qualifications of a scientific nature. However those in a managerial or supervisory role would normally have attended a HAZCHEM course. One major company, in fact, brought in experts to run such a course and also invited local firemen and Gardai to attend.

3.3.4 Gaps and Needs in the Existing Training Provision

Little was specified in the surveys on this topic. However, the same situation obtains as with road transport in that there is little specific training in hazardous wastes as such.

3.4 Transport by Inland Waterways

3.4.1 Existing Training Provision

Only Belgium, the Federal Republic of Germany and the Netherlands undertake significant transportation of hazardous substances by inland waterway.

Belgium has no specific regulations for the transportation of hazardous wastes as such but, if a boat is used to transport any hazardous substances, the owner must possess certain certificates of approval. While the regulations concerning safety at work apply, it is likely that boatmen who transport dangerous goods will soon have to possess a certificate showing a knowledge of the relevant regulations. Legislation on wastes also lays down certain general safety obligations.

The main German regulations concern the transportation of hazardous goods on the Rhine (the ADNR-Decree for implementation of the Decree relating to the transporting of hazardous goods on the Rhine and the extension thereof to other federal inland waterways). No specific education or training requirements are laid down for the crew, but there are certain general safety obligations to be observed during loading, discharge and handling. Although not yet a compulsory part of their training, crews do receive some information on hazardous substances at courses run by the Inland Navigation Professional Association at the three Federal German seamen's colleges. Management training for the Rhine includes 24 instruction units on the transportation of hazardous goods. Since 1st April 1989, a hazardous goods expert has been required on board whenever specific hazardous goods are being carried in quantities that exceed a specified level. Instruction is being provided for such experts, with an officially recognised examination and a refresher course every five years.

In the Netherlands there is no general professional training for inland navigation, although many shippers hold a long-distance certificate for inland navigation. Since 1st April 1989 it has been compulsory for everyone on board a ship sailing up and down the Rhine to have a valid ADNR certificate, renewable every five years.

A course organised by the Royal Shipping Training Fund deals with the transportation of dangerous substances by water. Again, no specific mention is made of chemical wastes.

3.5 Conclusions and recommendations

3.5.1 Conclusions

Road Transport

- Road transport is more frequently used than any other form of transport for the transportation of hazardous wastes.

- The educational background of most drivers is limited to basic school education plus, occasionally, some vocational training. Most drivers employed have some experience of driving.

- Most Member States stipulate training requirements for drivers of vehicles transporting hazardous substances. Sometimes this is for tanker drivers only: in other cases it covers all forms of hazardous goods transportation. All employers must also comply with national work safety legislation.

- At management level, the degree of educational qualification tends to vary with the size of the organisation.

- Most Member States apart from Greece have some form of required driver training, and much of the training is either for or approximately equivalent to that required for the International ADR certificate. Both external and in-house courses are run for this purpose. However, nearly all such training relates to hazardous substances in general and there is little training relating to the specific problems of hazardous wastes. Recognising the need, a number of organisations and companies are beginning to develop appropriate training courses.

- Difficulties are experienced by the smaller firms in some countries because of the degree of competition, the costs of training and the cost of employing drivers with better qualifications.

Rail Transport

- Rail transport is used to only a very limited extent in the transportation of hazardous wastes.

- None of the countries involved undertakes any training in the handling or management of hazardous wastes, although a limited degree of training on the carriage of dangerous goods in general does take place.

Sea Transport

- There is no legislation on the educational qualifications required of those involved in the transportation of hazardous wastes, although Captains and Officers will have been trained to a certain minimum level.

- There is no specific legislation regarding training for those involved in the transportation of hazardous wastes. Courses are available dealing with the handling of dangerous goods in general and Officer training usually incorporates some instruction in dangerous substances. German law does specify safety obligations when handling mixtures and solutions.

Transport by Inland Waterways

- There are no specific requirements regarding the education and training of those involved in the transportation of hazardous wastes by inland waterway. Such transportation would be covered by the various items of legislation concerning hazardous goods in general.

3.5.2 Recommendations

The following paragraphs summarise the specific recommendations made by individual countries.

- Training courses specifically geared to the transportation of hazardous wastes should be developed.

- Co-operation in training should be encouraged.

- Drivers should be retrained at intervals of less than five years to allow regular updating: training on hazardous wastes should be included in normal ADR training

- A professional profile should be established for specialist waste-disposal heavy goods drivers.

4.0 EDUCATION AND TRAINING OF PERSONNEL INVOLVED IN THE CLEAN-UP OF CONTAMINATED SOIL

4.1 The Approach to the Problem

Apart from Ireland, where large-scale industrialisation is a comparatively recent phenomenon, contaminated sites occur in significant numbers in most EC countries. However the approach to the problem varies. In Greece, for instance, the widespread practice of fly tipping wastes into streams, ravines and open areas has resulted in significant contamination of water bodies, groundwater and soil. Yet the lack of practical expertise or experience in investigating and assessing such sites has resulted in little being done either to rehabilitate affected areas or to implement appropriate planning controls to prevent any further escalation of the problem. A similar situation obtains in both Portugal and Spain. In Spain, however, the National Toxic and Dangerous Wastes Plan which has recently been drafted incorporates a programme for the rehabilitation of contaminated sites, with a total investment over the next five years of Ptas 5,000 million. The Plan gives no information on how the programme is to be conducted.

In certain Member States with a longer industrial history, the approach to the problem is little different. Neither Belgium nor Luxembourg has any specific legislation concerning contaminated sites. There is no national definition in either case nor any comprehensive inventory of sites. In Belgium it is compulsory for the operators of controlled landfill sites to restore the sites to their former condition on expiry or withdrawal of the authorisation. In Flanders, an Order of 30 July 1985 makes the Flemish Wastes Authority (OVAM) responsible, in the case of default by the operator, for the compulsory clean-up of landfill sites in cases where the situation poses a threat to human health or to the environment. In the Walloon Region, public grants can be allocated to local authorities for the acquisition, cleaning and reclamation of sites. Furthermore, by an order of 12 November 1987 on certain categories of waste, all operators or owners of sites where toxic or hazardous wastes are being or have been deposited, discharged or stored must provide the Wastes Management Division of the Walloon Region with all the information needed for an inventory and for the identification of the wastes.

In practice, action in the Walloon Region is limited to emergency measures after accidents. In Flanders, however, OVAM's Reseach and Technical Directorate has conducted 13 surveys of contaminated sites, most of which are complete.

Because, nationally, the demand from both public and private sectors is very small, no firm specialises in the clean-up of contaminated soil, although Serveco is occasionally involved in this work. One firm, Smet-Jet, is beginning to specialise in this field to meet the demand from the German market in particular.

Other countries have undertaken inventories. Germany, for instance, estimates that the number of contaminated sites is between 42,000 and 48,000, and that perhaps one in eight of these constitutes a high potential hazard. However, two specific problems face German companies involved in the clean-up of contaminated soil:

- the labour market does not make adequately qualified personnel available;

- there are no relevant legal standards.

Personnel are likely to come into contact with hazardous substances both during the initial risk assessment and during subsequent reclamation or securing measures. They may be affected by gas-release, by dust, by absorption through the skin or by explosions. Safety precautions are not always observed and, because many jobs go out to tender, many companies involved in the work are inadequately informed - partly because local authorities are themselves inadequately informed.

In the Netherlands it is recognised that it is impracticable to implement a single standard package of health and safety regulations for soil decontamination activities. This is principally because sites vary in terms of risk and scale, and therefore approaches to remediation and field practices will also vary.

In order to maintain adequate safety levels the draft publication "Working with Contaminated Soil" outlines two catergories of risk; toxicity and flammability. Separate protective measures have been laid down in each catergory. This approach also establishes a number of elementary rules which must always be observed in all decontamination procedures.

In the UK, the number of contaminated sites is estimated to be about 20,000 of which over 55% comprise disused gas works. The UK, alone among the 12 Member States, operates on the basis that public funds are a necessary requisite for the restoration of derelict land, including contaminated sites.

4.2 Background of Personnel Involved

Only six Member States are directly involved in the clean-up of contaminated soil. At Smet-Jet in Belgium, the minimum requirement for managers and non-manual workers is a degree or A1 diploma in chemistry. Similarly, skilled personnel are employed in Denmark for the investigation and assessment of contaminated sites and for subsequent management and supervision during clean-up. In the UK it is normal for a site investigation manager/supervisor to be qualified to at least degree level in engineering, geology, chemistry, biology or environmental science. It is not uncommon however, for project management to be undertaken by employees with post-graduate qualifications in these fields.

In the Netherlands, while project and site managers normally have third level academic or technical qualifications (usually in the construction field) and supervisors usually have second level qualifications in construction subjects, the Dutch classification of site risks in terms of toxicity (T) and flammability (F) has resulted in further stipulations. For example, sites involving risk category 1T are required to employ a consultant to minimise the chance of hazards being overlooked. As the risk levels increase, so do the personnel requirements. For work in Category 2T a safety expert/hygiene officer with knowledge and experience of first aid should be involved. For work in Category 3T, a safety expert/hygiene officer (or deputy) with third level technical qualifications and experience should be continuously on site while work is in progress. For work in Category 3F, an expert who is a qualified engineer should be attached to the operation.

For operatives, very little stipulation is made concerning basic qualifications. In the UK, most equipment operators, drivers and labourers only work intermittently on sites of this type and will have only the standard school education. Because, from 1989, all operators of earth-moving equipment have to be licensed, some staff in these categories will have attended the appropriate training courses prior to their employment on site. In other countries, too, operatives have only basic education, and there is some concern about their inadequate knowledge of chemicals. At Smet-Jet in Belgium, while there are no stipulations concerning starting qualifications, manual workers undergo a six-month trial period under the supervision of the 'product' managers.

In France the situation is somewhat different. Because the clean-up of contaminated sites is relatively uncommon, when it is undertaken the work is done by firms who either treat or dispose of hazardous wastes or collect and transport them - or both. The personnel involved simply adapt their knowledge and skills to the particular instance, paying special attention to identifying the wastes concerned. The small number of sites which are reclaimed by stabilisation/solidification techniques also involve specialist firms - usually engineering companies - with a small number of employees all highly educated in the engineering and technical fields. They are usually well informed about the safety problems likely to be encountered and are familiar with the use of protective masks, etc. Those bodies responsible for analysing and monitoring contaminated sites are again highly educated personnel in the engineering and technical field, though, in general, they will not have received training specifically concerned with working in hazardous conditions.

4.3 Existing Training Provision

There is no statutory obligation to provide training for those working on the clean-up of contaminated land beyond the national stipulations regarding safety in employment. In most countries involved in this work, employers are obliged to provide appropriate instructions and information as to the hazards involved and the need to use personal protection measures. Only in Denmark is there a statutory training requirement for those employed in the removal of material containing asbestos. A five-day course on asbestos removal is provided by the Labour Market Training System (the AMU). Further training opportunities are also provided for engineers and similarly qualified personnel under the Association of Danish Engineers' Further Training (DIEU). This includes the course 'Contaminated industrial and building sites'.

In the Netherlands the national regulations are contained in the Working Conditions Act and the decree based upon it which relates to safety in factories and places of work, and also in the Employment Act and the decree on the Employment of Young People which is based on it. Further Guidelines provided in a draft booklet 'Working with Contaminated Soil' are already being followed in practice.

Because of varying circumstances, it is impossible to design a single package of regulations. General regulations therefore stipulate that employees must be properly informed, in writing, at the start of each new job, of the nature of the work, of the risks entailed and of the rules to be observed. Further regulations are then dependent on the category of work involved. For all work in F Categories, for instance, employees directly concerned must be familiar with the use of the relevant fire extinguishers. Those who need to use breathing apparatus should be familiar with its use. For work in Category 2T, all employees working permanently on site and regularly entering the contaminated zone must attend a verbal information and instruction meeting arranged and given by either the site manager, the company medical officer and/or the safety expert/hygiene officer. A similar meeting should be arranged for all those in Category 3T work who regularly visit or who spend eight hours or more at a stretch in the contaminated zone. Simple protective clothing/equipment should be demonstrated and instructions given for its use.

The Dutch Institute for Working Conditions offers a course on healthy and safe working with contaminated land. This course is intended for site supervisors and was designed to enable them to recognise, at an early stage, the health risks involved in any soil decontamination project, to evaluate any risk of danger and to control such risks by taking effective precautions.

In Germany most training is in-house training and there is no independent and pertinent vocational training system available. Furthermore, such training as does exist involves only management. For instance, in one company interviewed, in-house seminars and meetings are arranged annually for senior site managers and site managers. Such meetings involve the exchange of information and experience, and external consultants provide reports on current topics such as contaminated land reclamation procedures. The Civil Engineering Professional Association offers an independent advanced training programme which includes lectures for site management personnel on the topic of 'health and safety at work during contaminated land reclamation'. To date, there has been only limited interest in this programme.

In the UK, most training can be described as 'on-the-job' training, for managers and operatives alike. No formal training in contaminated land investigation is likely: those undertaking this work acquire the appropriate knowledge in relation to hazard recognition, safety procedures and supervisory duties as a result of work experience and contact with fellow professionals. Operative training again is through individual work experience and on-the-job instruction.

Loughborough University does offer a course covering investigation, assessment, legislative controls, remediation options, etc. This is in no sense a beginners' course, and those attending include local authority planning officers, environmental health officers and employees of companies involved in site investigation and land development.

By way of contrast, Smet-Jet of Belgium, a company which has only recently become involved in this area of work, is developing a rather more sophisticated training scheme. Technical, commercial, safety and soil-reclamation training is given to the whole of the sales and operations team, including all operatives apart from those on the commercial side. Training is continuous to take into account changes and new developments. All training is filmed on video cassettes, watched by those concerned and then discussed. In addition there is a practical training element. The Fire Brigade provide a training course on the more practical aspects of working in unhealthy places, including putting out fires, cleaning lorries, wearing masks etc. Practical training exercises on cleaning have been introduced and practical training on soil clean-up is planned.

Every worker is given a work card for each day. This card lists the jobs to be done and the safety measures to be taken. Any accidents that occur are discussed by works committees and by the site superintendent with the person causing the accident.

Managers of the strategy division attend external seminars, and everyone is involved in continuous training by staff supervision.

4.4 Gaps and Needs in the Existing Training Provision

It is evident from the above (apart from Smet-Jet), not only that training specifically aimed at those working on the clean-up of contaminated soils is limited, but that such training as there is is geared to middle and senior management and not to those actually undertaking the work on site.

4.5 Conclusions and Recommendations

4.5.1 Conclusions

- Very few Member States have an accurate inventory of sites contaminated with hazardous wastes.
- Only six Member States are directly involved in the clean-up of contaminated soil to any significant extent.

- Management and supervisory staff are normally qualified to the equivalent of degree level, the levels required depending to some extent on the degree of hazard involved.

- Operatives have normally only completed the basic school education.

- There is no statutory obligation to provide training for those working on the clean-up of contaminated land, although national health and safety regulations apply for the protection of employees.

- Denmark and the Netherlands both offer courses on working with contaminated land. In Germany and the UK, most training takes place on the job, although Loughborough University in the UK does offer a relevant advanced course. Smet-Jet in Belgium has developed its own sophisticated in-house training scheme. Most of the external courses available are geared to middle and senior management.

4.5.2 Recommendations

The following paragraphs summarise the specific recommendations made by individual countries.

- More training provision is needed for 'shop-floor' personnel

- Additional courses are required at the decision-making level.

- More practical training is needed to provide a better knowledge of chemicals.

5.0 EDUCATION AND TRAINING IN RELATION TO THE DUTIES AND RESPONSIBILITIES OF REGULATORY AGENCIES

5.1 Introduction

Under the EC Directive on toxic and dangerous waste, Member States are required to designate or establish competent authorities which will be responsible for the planning, organisation, authorisation and supervision of operations for the disposal of hazardous wastes.

These bodies are required to understand all the technical, environmental, health and administration aspects involved in the day-to day management of hazardous waste.

5.2 Responsible Bodies

5.2.1 Belgium

The main responsible bodies in Belgium for administering and monitoring the standards relating to the management of wastes are, in Flanders, the Flemish Wastes Authority (OVAM) and, in the Walloon Region, the Wastes Management and Pollution Prevention Departments of the Ministry of the Walloon Region. These two Walloon departments will eventually be transferred to the Walloon Wastes Office once this is established.

The international movement of wastes is the responsibility of the Environment Unit of the Ministry of Public Health and the Environment, while responsibility for monitoring the transportation of dangerous goods by road is in the hands of a specially trained police force of the Ministry of Communications. Antwerp has its own Environmental Police Force and the Maritime Inspectorate is based at the same port.

5.2.2 Denmark

Government, regional and municipal authorities are all responsible to some degree for monitoring the management of hazardous wastes, as is the Labour Inspectorate. Company Health Services, which according to the legislation must be established at certain types of industries or as 'centres' serving a group of such industries, have more advisory than enforcement powers.

5.2.3 France

In France, the survey identified three responsible groups likely to be involved in monitoring the management of hazardous wastes:

- Inspectors of Classified Plants, who monitor the general safety of plants and their environments and who act on behalf of the Ministry of the Environment;

- Labour Inspectors, who are responsible for ensuring that the provisions of the Labour Code are applied;

- Inspectors employed by the Regional Sickness-Insurance Offices (CRAM), whose role is to promote and co-ordinate measures to prevent industrial accidents and occupational illnesses.

5.2.4 Germany

The situation in Germany is complicated by the fact that bodies with responsibility for special waste and for contaminated land are divided into a large number of different departments. Differences also exist between Provinces. In North Rhine-Westphalia alone, responsibilities in the special waste sector are divided between two provincial ministries, five district government bodies, two provincial departments, eight national government departments for water and waste, 22 trade supervisory offices, 12 local mining authorities and 54 districts and autonomous municipalities. Furthermore, the bodies mentioned are only responsible for the more important planning, licensing and supervisory tasks.

Because of increased public awareness and legislation in this sector, there has been a wave of administrative and organisational reforms and changes, and new departments have been created. Problems do still exist, however, notably with staffing.

5.2.5 Greece

The competent bodies responsible for the safe disposal of waste in Greece are Local Boroughs, District Authorities, Development Agencies or Municipal Enterprises. Port Authorities are responsible for waste generated at sea.

However, the monitoring of handling and management of wastes is complicated by the large number of organisations involved (at all levels) which leads to administrative confusion and inefficiency. There are too few personnel with adequate training, and there is a shortage of appropriate equipment. Furthermore, there is little general awareness on the part of local officials of the environmental hazards resulting from inappropriate hazardous waste collection and disposal.

5.2.6 Ireland

Only a small number of Local Authorities in Ireland are involved on any scale in regulating the disposal and treatment of toxic wastes. These include Cork and Dublin and, to a lesser extent, Limerick and Clare. Toxic waste facilities are visited regularly but, as the waste is mostly exported, samples are not normally taken for analysis apart from effluent samples.

5.2.7 Luxembourg

The Wastes Division of the Department of the Environment is mainly responsible for the problems of hazardous waste, and has a staff comprising three full-time officials, and three more on fixed-term contracts.

Other experts and agents likely to play a part in the relevant monitoring include the Mines and Factories Inspectorate (with responsibility within firms), the Water and Forests Administration, and the Testing and Control Laboratories Division of the Agricultural Technical Services Administration.

5.2.8 Netherlands

Three bodies in the Netherlands have responsibilities in this sector.

- Officials of the Inspectorate of Labour ensure that the provisions of the Working Conditions Act and its associated legal regulations are observed: their work involves the investigation of offences, the provision of advice and information, and the issuing of warnings, demands and closure orders.

- The Central Inspectorate and regional inspectors of the Public Health Inspectorate (Environmental Inspection) come under the Directorate General of Environmental Protection of the Ministry of Housing, Physical Planning and the Environment (VROM): their work involves advising the Minister on matters of public health, advising Local Authorities under various Environmental Acts, appealing, where considered necessary, against environmental permits, and investigating offences involving pollution.

In 1984, as a result of an Extended Intensification Programme on the implementation of the Chemical Waste Act (CWA), considerable attention was paid to education and information in connection with implementing the legislation relating to chemical waste. This includes the provision of information and publicity material to companies, and it is suggested that this should be part of normal inspection duties.

- Inspectors of Hazardous Substances are an independent force, and part of the Ministry of Transport, Water Control and Public Works. They ensure the observance of transport regulations for hazardous substances including waste, and spend a considerable amount of time on training and retraining as well as inspection. They work closely with the Police Central Traffic Committee and with the Central Council on Water Safety.

5.2.9 Spain

Responsible bodies for the monitoring of hazardous waste management in Spain operate at both the national and the local level.

At the national level, central administration lies with the Ministry of Public Works and Town and Country Planning (MOPU), and more specifically with the Department of the Environment and the Wastes Service of the Directorate General for the Environment within MOPU. MOPU is responsible for

- co-ordinating hazardous waste policy at the national level;
- co-ordinating the activities relating to hazardous waste where they affect more than one Autonomous Community;
- imposing penalties;
- co-ordinating Spanish policy on toxic and dangerous wastes with policies of Member States and other non-member countries.

The Autonomous Communities work at the local level through the appropriate services (eg Wastes Services) and departments. The Environmental Department is responsible for monitoring hazardous waste management, inspecting plants, proposing penalties and supplying MOPU with information.

The transportation of waste is under the jurisdiction of the environmental authorities and the Ministry of Transport.

5.2.10 United Kingdom

The Waste Disposal Authority (WDA) is the main organisation involved in the day-to-day management and regulation of hazardous wastes in the UK. The Health and Safety Executive and Environmental Health Officers are involved when issues of public or worker health have been raised. WDA officers are responsible for the drawing up and enforcement of conditions attached to site licences. They also act as advisers to industry and make recommendations on the handling, treatment and disposal of wastes:

an additional role is in administering the consignment note procedure which is used to monitor and approve the disposal of hazardous waste. Officers may operate alone or as part of a team of specialists.

Her Majesty's Inspectorate of Pollution (HMIP) which now incorporates the Hazardous Waste Inspectorate has no statutory role in the management of hazardous waste, though it does advise on standards of practice and policy in this area.

5.3 Background of Personnel Involved

5.3.1 Belgium

The Flemish Wastes Authority (OVAM) employs Grade 1 civil servants for management and staff supervision. These staff normally have degrees or university-level diplomas in various fields. Administrators are normally Grade 2 civil servants with higher secondary level diplomas, often in environmental subjects.

The Pollution Prevention Department of the Ministry of the Walloon Region employs Grade 1 civil servants who are usually chemists, technicians, or civil or industrial engineers. In the Wastes Management Department, only seven Grade 1 civil servants are employed, the remainder of the staff being contract workers and people with higher and lower secondary education diplomas.

The Environment Unit of the Ministry of Public Health and the Environment uses mainly contract workers and unemployed persons: as a result, qualifications rarely match the jobs undertaken.

The Management Unit for the Mathematical Model of the North Sea, which undertakes the computerised monitoring of dumping at sea, consists entirely of graduates, most of them scientists.

Overall, however, there is difficulty in recruiting highly qualified staff, as the public sector offers less pay and fewer opportunities than many other sectors of the economy.

5.3.2 Denmark

Like Belgium, the authorities involved in the management of waste disposal usually require their staff to have a minimum level of training as engineers, biologists, lawyers etc. The Labour Inspectorate and Company Health Services usually employ engineers together with technical staff such as machine operators, work environment technicians, and nurses.

5.3.3 France

In France, all inspectors in this area of work have a high level of education - mainly university degrees or engineering diplomas. Such qualifications are a condition of recruitment. Those inspectors working with the Regional Sickness-Insurance Offices (CRAM) have usually had previous experience in industry and are skilled in issues relating to personal safety. In all fields, however, it is a case of highly qualified staff adapting their skills to deal with hazardous waste.

5.3.4 Germany

Because of the large number of different departments involved in the management and monitoring of hazardous wastes, the number of personnel involved is substantial and the level of formal qualifications is varied. Because of tight budgets and staff economy measures, the situation exists where fewer staff are required to do a greater variety of jobs whatever their existing level of qualification.

5.3.5 Greece

The survey revealed that, in Greece, many regulatory officers are educated to diploma level, a level regarded as 'higher' than that of a UK degree because it satisfies not only academic, but also professional requirements.

5.3.6 Ireland

As in other Member States, most Local Authority officers involved in the management and monitoring of hazardous waste normally have degrees in chemistry or in chemical or civil engineering.

5.3.7 Luxembourg

The Wastes Division of the Department of the Environment employs mainly chemists, including two higher ranking civil servants. The Mines and Factorie Inspectorate also has higher (including technical and chemical engineers) as well as middle and lower ranking civil servants. The one medical officer in the Factories Inspectorate has degrees in industrial medicine and industrial toxicology.

5.3.8 Netherlands

Officers in the Environmental Inspectorate are usually qualified to degree level. While Inspectors of Hazardous Substances, who ensure observance of transport regulations for hazardous substances, including wastes, must hold the Police Diploma A and have completed five years in the Police Force before they are admitted.

5.3.9 Spain

The recent date of the legislation coupled with a poor response to the survey means that little information is available about the background of personnel involved in this area of work. However, as in most other countries, there is a tendency for responsible personnel to have higher education qualifications in subjects such as chemistry, engineering and biology.

5.3.10 UK

There is no educational or work experience background which is typical of Waste Disposal Authority officers. Many transfer from other areas of Local Government, for instance Surveyors' or Environmental Health Departments. Their educational background may vary from basic secondary education to degree level qualifications. More recent recruits are more likely to come from colleges or universities, and mostly from science and technical courses such as chemistry, geology, civil engineering or environmental science. Many WDAs employ people from both university and industry.

5.4 Existing Training Provision

5.4.1 Belgium

No statutory training is laid down for officers responsible for administering and monitoring the standards relating to the management of hazardous wastes, apart from those relevant to all employees at work. Most training, throughout Belgium, is on-the-job training, and the only course (outside police colleges) for civil servants responsible for monitoring and enforcing environmental laws is the 'Policing the Environment' course at Antwerp University, which commenced in 1989. There is, however, a project for integrating training in environmental policing practice being managed by the Institut des Affaires Publiques at Charleroi. The aim of this venture is to enable regions, provinces and communes to train their personnel to manage the various problems connected with the environment. The 'nuisance-wastes' module devised within this project is designed to last for five days.

In Flanders, all civil servants are required to study the legislation and have two to three months of instruction by supervision before working in the field. The Nuclear Energy Centre at Mol also helps to train civil servants at seminars organised within OVAM, and various external seminars and training days are held.

In the Walloon Region there are too few staff to permit frequent attendance at external seminars, and so on-the-job training under supervision is backed up by the circulation of texts of regulations. It is, however, by no means certain that these are always read.

5.4.2 Denmark

Danish law has no specific requirements for the training of personnel in this area of work, and only the Work Environment Act applies. Training opportunities are, however, provided for authorities involved in the management of wastes disposal by Kommunekemi, the Municipal College, the Association of Danish Engineers' Further Training (DIEU) and the Technological Institute. Courses for the Labour Inspectorate and Company Health Services are offered within the Labour Market Training System, and by the Labour Inspectorate itself (internal courses).

5.4.3 France

All Inspectors in France are given information and general training in the problems of industrial risks, and this is adapted to suit the specific nature of their tasks. Special information activities may be organised for Inspectors of Classified Plants at the regional or the national level, but there is no general or systematic training in issues relating to hazardous wastes. CRAM and Labour Inspectors receive special safety training which is provided by the National Institute of Research and Safety but, again, this does not necessarily deal specifically with hazardous wastes.

5.4.4 Germany

In Germany there is no special training for 'licensing and supervision'. Either staff are trained by the authorities themselves, or graduates from civil service training colleges become qualified by means of special training (technical and/or in natural sciences), usually through the quaternary education sector. In some cases, staff with the appropriate technical training are recruited and then provided with the necessary advanced administrative training.

Because the technical qualifications required are the same as those required by the companies being supervised, there is competition for staff, and civil service departments may have difficulty in recruiting suitable staff because of the lower financial incentives they can offer.

Some special programmes are available, for instance 'Environmental hygiene in the public health sector': this is aimed at personnel in the public health field and includes the problems surrounding (special) waste. There are also training programmes for specific target groups such as hygiene nurses, health supervisors and medical practitioners in public health. All these programmes consider the problems of special wastes.

There are also a number of specialist advanced training courses for the staff of licensing and supervisory authorities which are run by central departments of the Federal Provinces. For instance, there is an advanced training seminar for responsible municipal officers on the problems of contaminated land. And the Federal Office for Water and Waste has included a programme on contaminated land in its advanced instructor training course for those who train suppliers and disposers of waste.

5.4.5 Greece

The regulatory officers, already described above as highly qualified, undertake further training on the job and through a series of seminars and workshops organised by Central Government. In addition, they may attend conferences and seminars held in other Member States.

5.4.6 Ireland

There is no organised training programme for those environmental engineers responsible for enforcing legislation. All training is done on the job. There are occasional one-day conferences on special topics and, at Government Department level, the staff involved are likely to have attended courses on toxic waste matters at Harwell in England.

Because of the low priority given to training, the Irish authorities depend heavily on outside agencies such as the Environmental Services Group of the Irish Science and Technology Agency (EOLAS) to set standards for the handling of toxic waste. The standards and controls are set at the planning stage, and policing is by default, i.e. direct intervention only occurs as a result of an incident.

5.4.7 Italy

Educational courses for monitoring personnel are usually broadly based and carried out at the central and local level. There are no specific courses in the hazardous wastes sector, but certain regions such as Lombardy organise annual specialist training courses for managers of public health, environmental health and the protection of health in the workplace.

5.4.8 Luxembourg

As in other Member States, there is no specific legal or regulatory requirement relating to the training of civil servants or state employees who are involved in monitoring the management of hazardous waste. Neither is there any specific training programme for civil servants on environmental matters. Training is generally acquired by on-the-job experience, although some officials do attend seminars or conferences abroad. The Ministry of the Environment has recently held a course on the disposal of PCBs which was open to all government employees as well as to industrialists. The Medical Officer of the Factories Inspectorate undertakes regular refresher courses.

5.4.9 Netherlands

Those employed by the Environmental Inspectorate spend about 5% of their working hours on educational activities which form part of a training programme. This involves both training in the necessary skills and courses on relevant subjects.

The Environmental Inspectorate also organises courses in collaboration with police organisations, schools of management and other educational institutions for those who supervise and implement environmental regulations. In 1987, about 1,000 people completed a course on the Chemical Wastes Act (CWA). In 1986 and 1987, 800 or so supervisors completed a course on 'The Sampling and Analysis of Chemical Waste. This course was run under the auspices of the Environmental Inspectorate in collaboration with TAUW Infra Consult, and a major component was the identification, properties and safety aspects of chemical wastes. A further course has also been prepared to train those outside the Inspectorate who are responsible for implementing regulations under the CWA. This aims to increase knowledge of the relevant technical, legal and chemical aspects. Courses are also provided for police and Local Authority officials with supervisory duties.

In addition to the courses, instruction and publicity materials relating to the technical and safety aspects of chemical wastes are distributed. The Environmental Inspectorate also makes many contributions to postgraduate courses and other courses on environmental pollution.

Inspectors of hazardous substances, who ensure observance of transport regulations, undertake in-house training including a study of the law. Most of their training is of a practical nature. As well as inspection work, much of their time is spent on training and retraining others, although this Inspectorate does not provide courses. Little specific attention is, however, given to the dangerous properties of hazardous wastes.

5.4.10 Portugal

A number of agencies are involved in work safety and in the training of work-safety officers, and particular mention should be made of the training activities organised by the Institute of Employment and Vocational Training. A number of public health courses also exist. None of these courses, however, are specifically related to the monitoring of hazardous waste management.

5.4.11 Spain

No wastes-training programmes have yet been set up in Spain, although occasional courses and seminars (usually of a very general nature) do take place and are attended by a limited number of personnel. Most training is based on work experience and self-education from specialist books and reviews.

5.4.12 UK

Experience is considered to be a vital part of training in the UK. The result, however, is a lack of standardisation. The Department of the Environment has made some attempt to minimise the effect of local variations in practice and policy by producing a series of Waste Management Papers. This has not been entirely successful and new and ammended Papers have recently been published.

Employees with a skills shortage are encouraged to attend a relevant training course. For instance, in one Waste Disposal Authority, junior employees lacking a background in Chemistry are required to study for a Higher National Certificate in chemistry.

Courses attended by WDA officers include the Diploma in Waste Management, introductory and advanced courses in Hazardous Waste Management and various NAWDC courses. In addition, numerous one-day seminars and courses are organised by various institutions.

A major problem, particularly for some of the smaller WDAs, is the cost and time involved in staff attending such courses.

5.5 Gaps and Needs in the Existing Training Provision

Inevitably, the gaps and needs in the existing training provision will vary from country to country, but a number of conclusions can be drawn from the surveys undertaken.

Several countries experienced a lack of training infrastructure. Belgium, for instance, was reported as lacking programmes, funds, an appropriate administrative structure, qualified instructors and training equipment. The Danish report, too, noted a lack of resources for advanced problem evaluation/solving, while training provision in Spain is poor, with only a few courses of a general nature.

In Greece, the limited investment in waste handling and treatment to date has resulted in the suggestion that technical environmental advisers should be attached to local communities. Some of these would be specialists and would be located in the larger communities and advise on such matters as solid wastes, hazardous wastes, sewage treatment and water supply. In addition, there is a requirement for some 1,300 special waste management advisers. These should be young engineering graduates who would then follow a three-month theoretical and practical training with an emphasis on hazardous waste.

In Luxembourg, the small numbers involved in this work suggests that training should be undertaken abroad. However, the country does have a government training institute; the infrastructure is therefore there and courses could be developed.

One of the problems in Germany is the fragmented nature of responsibility. There is an excessively specialised and detailed allocation of tasks which results in only a selective perception of problems by individuals, a problem exacerbated by a lack of co-operation and exchange of information between departments. There is a deficient knowledge of regulations and basic facts on the part of officials. There is gross understaffing and a lack of advanced training. There is therefore a need for a training system which allows personnel to identify a problem and evaluate its ramifications. Furthermore, advanced training should be linked with salaries and opportunities for promotion.

In some countries where a training infrastructure does exist, the smaller authorities may find it difficult to release staff, either because of the costs involved, or because of understaffing. This can certainly happen in both Belgium, Ireland and the UK.

Much of the foregoing relates to general training. It is evident from the surveys that there are very few courses available which are specifically geared to hazardous waste management, and this is the major problem.

5.6 Conclusions and Recommendations

5.6.1 Conclusions

- Those organisations responsible for administering and monitoring the standards applied to the management of hazardous waste are clearly defined in most Member States. However, in Germany and Greece, monitoriing is complicated by the division of responsibility between large numbers of different departments.

- In most Member States a high proportion of those involved in inspection and monitoring the management of hazardous wastes are graduates or senior civil servants with qualifications in such subjects as chemistry, engineering and biology. This particularly applies to senior posts. In Germany, however, because of the large number of different departments responsible for this work, the number of personnel involved is substantial and their qualifications are varied.

- Training provision varies from country to country. There are no statutory regulations regarding training in this area of work, but most countries accept the importance of training even if, in practice, this is restricted to training on the job. There is no systematic training in issues relating to hazardous wastes for staff in any Member State. However, external courses which contain relevant elements are offered in most of the more industrialised countries. In addition, seminars or conferences on topics of relevance may be held.

- The main problems encountered in the provision of appropriate training are the lack of resources (funds, qualified instructors, equipment etc), lack of an adequate infrastructure in certain Member States, and understaffing with its associated difficulties of releasing staff for training.

- The main need is for appropriate courses to be developed.

5.6.2 Recommendations

The following paragraphs summarise the specific recommendations made by individual countries.

- Training should be improved, particularly in terms of knowledge of legislation, administrative and judiciary procedures of wastes management and safety. Resources therefore need to be made available.

- There is a need for more specialist waste management courses to be developed in order to ensure responsible officers are kept up to date on technological developments affecting the nature and generation of industrial waste and on new developments within the waste disposal industry.

- Regional co-ordination of training should take place where appropriate in order to encourage participation and reduce costs.

- Resources for setting up and participating in training corses on hazardous wastes need to be made available.

6.0 EDUCATION AND TRAINING OF THOSE IN THE EMERGENCY SERVICES IN RELATION TO HAZARDOUS WASTE

6.1 Integration of the Emergency Services in Relation to Hazardous Waste

In several countries co-operation between the various emergency services is well organised. In Spain, for instance, the civil defence organisation is responsible for overall control in the case of a national emergency while in more localised incidents either the local civil defence or the fire services may have overall responsibility. This does not, however, apply specifically to emergencies involving hazardous wastes.

In France, there is a statutory requirement for establishments handling hazardous waste to establish both an interior operations plan (POI) and a special intervention plan (PPI). The former relates to the internal safety of a plant and to internal action to be taken in the event of an accident. The latter relates to the intervention of external emergency services in the event of an accident. These plans must, of course, be co-ordinated. The emergency services involved, however, do not necessarily receive specific training in relation to hazardous wastes.

In Germany, no differentiation is made between hazardous wastes amd hazardous substances in general. There is great emphasis on co-operation between the emergency services, which are interconnected by telephone and, often, radio. In Belgium too emergency plans are drawn up by civil defence and fire services and also by some industries. The 'BIG' computer system provides immediate technical information for those dealing with chemical hazards.

6.2 Medical, Nursing and Paramedical Staff

In most Member States, it is rare for doctors and nurses to be involved at incidents unless there are large numbers of casualties or unless the incident is located at a plant with its own works medical section. Perhaps the main exception to this is the Federal German Republic where a Professional Association of Emergency Doctors exists.

Emergency Doctors in Germany qualify as such when they can offer the following:

- a licence to practise as a doctor;

- one year's clinical service in the practice of intensive medicine;

- proof of five instances of having implemented life-saving measures as an assistant to an emergency doctor;

- proof of successful attendance at three courses in emergency medicine, with a total of 60 hours' instruction. These courses normally include simulations of typical situations involving hazardous substances.

Senior emergency doctor training, for co-ordination and leadership in major accident situations, is open to those with at least three years' experience as an emergency doctor, plus a third year of training as a specialist in surgery, anaesthesia or internal medicine. At no point, however, is there any specific training for coping with the effects of hazardous wastes, although courses run by the Professional Association do, in certain areas, touch on this subject.

The training of medical and nursing staff in all countries tends to focus on the treatment of casualties. Sometimes relevant information is available for the treatment of chemically exposed casualties. For instance, the Poison Information Centre at Beaumont Hospital, Dublin, has an advisory service which is manned day and night by specially trained staff.

Works medical officers are inevitably involved in emergency situations when incidents occur at their place of work. In Belgium, works medical officers are doctors of medicine with special training in industrial medicine, including in-depth courses on occupational toxicology. Medical officers in the Factory Inspectorate are also doctors, in some cases with certificates in industrial medicine. Both groups take part in seminars and training days on various topics.

Both company doctors and the medical officer of the FactoriesInspectorate in Luxembourg must have successfully completed at least two years' specialist training in industrial medicine. All training is undertaken abroad, although certain private industrial medicine assocations do organise occasional seminars on topics relating to industrial toxicology or safety. Larger firms with their own medical departments organise refresher courses on topics specific to the firm. In this they are supported by the Ministry of Health.

The Portuguese National School of Public Health also runs courses in industrial medicine, diagnostics and therapeutics.

The main role of the ambulance service is to provide first aid and transport to hospital. Paramedic/ambulance training varies considerably from country to country. In Ireland, for instance, staff, who are recruited with at least secondary level education, undergo six weeks' training of which only two hours is devoted to chemical hazards. In the UK, some instruction is given on hazard identification and the use of breathing apparatus, and refresher courses are provided every 3-5 years.

In Germany, paramedic/ambulance attendant training has considerably improved since the beginning of 1989. The existing 560-hour training plus examination for an ambulance attendant has now been replaced by paramedic training lasting 1600 hours. This should extend the range of tasks they can perform with some legal safeguards.

In Luxembourg, ambulance personnel must hold a certificate awarded by the Civil Defence Directorate or some equivalent qualification. The National Civil Defence College organises a training weekend for first aid/ambulance volunteers, and they are also obliged to attend 16 two-hour training sessions at various emergency centres. The programme of training is adapted and improved each year to meet new problems.

6.3 Fire Brigade

In a number of Member States, the fire-fighting services are regarded as the key emergency service. They are often given the management role in any incident. For instance, in the UK, their management tasks are to safeguard life and to reduce or remove the hazard using a variety of safety equipment, clothing and machinery. For this, a thorough practical and theoretical training is necessary, provided in this instance by regional training centres and by the individual brigade headquarters.

In most countries, the degree of training depends on whether the service is a voluntary one or a professional one. In Luxembourg, for instance, apart from 110 full-time professional members of the Luxembourg City fire brigade, all other fire fighters are volunteers, managed by the local authorities.

Full-time recruits are required to be of an appropriate age and level of physical fitness and have achieved a certain academic/vocational level. They must pass an initial entrance examination and undergo two years' theoretical and practical training before their final examination and appointment. Subsequent training, usually by supervisors but occasionally externally (and even abroad), takes place in specialist areas of work - first aid, fire-fighting and lifesaving. At present there is only very rudimentary instruction on chemical hazards, but with slightly greater detail on hydrocarbon pollution. At the time of the survey, two senior firemen were undergoing training at the inter-regional fire-brigade training school at Metz in France on chemical hazards in industry and on the transportation of hazardous products and wastes.

Volunteers undertake voluntary training weekends at the National Fire Service College.

Belgium has 15-16,000 firemen, including 4,500 professionals. Admission criteria to the service are low in practice, and training courses vary regionally although most have established final examinations before certificates are granted. No courses have been designed specifically for dealing with hazardous wastes, although some courses for the certificate of Professional Officer deal more or less directly with chemical accidents, and firemen, especially in areas such as Antwerp and Liege do receive some instruction relating to hazardous substances. Overall, there is a lack of suitable equipment for dealing with hazardous substances, and where particular hazards are involved, specialist private firms are often called in.

Dutch fire service training includes more courses on dangerous substances although nothing specifically on chemical wastes. The two course modules on dangerous materials given to firemen and team leaders were standardised in May 1989, and include the identification and properties of dangerous materials, and the immediate action required. In addition, a national working group has put together a handbook of guidelines for dealing with incidents involving hazardous substances. Some companies, including 5% of CWA permit holders, have their own fire services. These are not only trained to a level equivalent to that achieved by the municipal fire services, but they also have their own in-house training courses geared to company needs. However, there is still a need for more specialists in dangerous substances.

Concern about the risks involved with chemical substances has resulted in some level of appropriate training in most courses. In Ireland, for instance, as well as some training in chemical safety in the basic courses, senior officers undergo two weeks of training on hazardous chemicals. In Italy, the General Command of the Fire Service, with its Headquarters in Rome, has established an information base which is useful for its work in chemical plants and at the scene of transport accidents involving dangerous substances, including wastes. Furthermore, courses and seminars are organised in conjunction with personnel from Federchemica (the chemical industry federation), the Montedison Company and ENI. Some of these courses deal with particular toxic products such as arsenic, chlorine and hydrogen, while others deal with the analysis of industrial risks.

The survey for Greece revealed an apparently highly developed approach to the whole question of hazardous substances. It was reported that each local station has officers trained to deal with situations arising out of accidents involving hazardous wastes or chemicals. They are reported to be capable of recognising the measures that need to be taken to prevent escalation, explosion or the generation or spread of poisonous fumes, but only if the relevant information is available - only, for instance, if a vehicle in an accident is correctly labelled with the chemical carried. All grades have received training in the basic principles of firefighting and in general physics and chemistry. Senior Fire Officers have received not only management training but also more detailed training in chemical spillages, major fires and explosions. Day release workshops and longer seminars are organised in specialist subjects to meet particular needs and, as in Rome, an information centre is being established within the Fire Service

Headquarters. This will contain information on the properties and behaviour of chemicals and will operate similarly to the UK HAZCHEM service.

In the UK, in order to fulfill their duties, all fire officers must undergo a thorough training programme. This focuses on practical aspects, e.g. methods of containing neutralising and cleaning up chemicals and wastes, reducing fire risks, using breathing apparatus, other equipment and first aid. The nature of dangerous substances, labelling and administrative systems are also covered.

Fire services in the Federal Republic of Germany are the responsibility of local authorities. Provincial training colleges and the fire services themselves provide the basic training. For Professional firemen, a maximum of 10% of their training is related to combating the risks of hazardous substances, and this is restricted to the provision of individual items of knowledge. Voluntary firemen, because of the more limited training time involved, have a much more elementary knowledge of such substances. About 10% of senior officers are chemical engineers who can contribute specialist knowledge about hazardous substances. However, all personnel of senior rank are provided with the necessary knowledge to allow them to make an accurate evaluation of the hazards of a given situation. Some fire services engage chemical specialists.

In addition to the standard training at each level, courses dealing with hazardous materials are provided by all provincial organisations for senior officers and for crews managing hazardous substance equipment. In general, there is plenty of opportunity for further training. The main difficulty is releasing the personnel to attend them.

The larger brigades have access to data banks and information systems as well as contacts with external analysis companies. These facilities enable them to deal with the problems posed by hazardous wastes. However, there is little training or information specifically on hazardous wastes.

6.4 Police

The role of the police in incidents involving hazardous wastes or hazardous substances in general varies considerably from country to country. In the Netherlands, for instance, the police are concerned with public order and not public safety. Although some attention is paid to hazardous substances in general during their training, the need exists for a better knowledge of chemicals, particularly on the part of the river police who may be investigating cases of pollution.

In Luxembourg, the educational standard for entry into the Gendarmerie and police service is not very high, and the one-year training course, although containing some details of the legislation relating to environmental protection, makes no reference to dealing with hazardous wastes.

In Ireland, on the other hand, there is a two-year training course for the Gardai which includes a small component relating to chemical safety at accidents, and six days per year are devoted to further training, mainly in the details of new legislation. Many Gardai have undergone a four-day HAZCHEM safety course, but they are rarely equipped with suitable protective clothing or trained in the use of breathing apparatus, and generally rely on the fire service to direct them at incidents.

Police training in Germany includes elements which are relevant to accidents involving hazardous wastes, and all Provinces offer a one-week seminar on environmental protection and on the penal code relating to the environment. However, any more specialist seminars on hazardous goods and special wastes are absent from the training. Some of the higher provincial colleges offer courses for middle and higher ranks on the supervision of special types of traffic, but only Bavaria and Baden-Wurttemberg have special hazardous goods supervision squads. The Trade Unions are currently requesting a training component on hazardous goods as a compulsory part of police education.

Rather more attention is paid to the question of hazardous wastes in the training and operation of police in Belgium and the UK although, in Belgium, training courses do vary considerably. The province of Luxembourg includes environmental issues in its basic training with a course on environmental law and a short review of legislation on wastes. The Limburg Police Study and Training Centre offers courses on wastes legislation in basic training for middle ranks (inspectors) and officers (superintendents), and continuing training on this topic is also planned for all officers. The Antwerp Police College provides a major training programme in environmental practices. This included, in 1989, a specific course on hazardous wastes. It also offers, as an advanced course for police officers, a 'Policing the Environment' course, organised in 1989 by Antwerp University.

Concern for the environment has resulted in the establishment of an 'Environment Police' division in Antwerp commune. This can take samples and conduct pollution measurements and is responsible for policing operating permits, the compulsory declarations that have to be made by hazardous waste producers and, in the case of trans-frontier movements, the incineration of wastes at sea, the transportation of hazardous substances etc. A similar Environment Division exists within the Copenhagen Police Force in Denmark. An internal course is provided on the transportation of dangerous goods, and training includes information relating to hazardous substances.

The gaps that do exist in training provision in this area largely result from the lack of any statutory obligation to provide such courses and also from the lack of standardisation of police college courses (currently under investigation). There is a definite need for all police to undergo simple training courses including examples and practical exercises. Training must also be regularly updated with refresher courses.

In the UK, officer training related to the transportation of hazardous wastes and dangerous goods is organised through County Constabularies. The police have two roles in relation to hazardous substances. They act as the eyes and ears of the Health and Safety Executive and therefore need to be familiar with the legislation and aware of the hazards posed by dangerous substances; and they are involved in supervising incidents during the transportation of hazardous goods. Training of supervisory ranks is more comprehensive. Although the training is not specifically related to hazardous wastes, these substances are considered.

6.5 Civil Defence Organisations

In a number of countries, the civil defence organisations have an important role to play in emergency situations. Belgium has five permanent civil defence units located throughout the country, each managed by an industrial engineer. All staff are subject to the staff regulations for state employees and also undertake training courses and examinations organised by the Royal Civil Defence School. No specific training is provided on hazardous wastes, but certain courses, albeit not very advanced ones, do relate directly to accidents caused by chemical products.

Training in the four civil defence units which come under Luxembourg's Ministry of the Interior has more emphasis on nuclear hazards and hydrocarbon pollution than on chemical accidents, and no information is provided on hazardous wastes.

In Spain, it is the Civil Defence that is responsible for taking action in an emergency, disaster etc. Its organisational structure covers the whole country, and a centralised management is responsible for co-ordinating all branches and any other emergency services that may need to be involved. In more localised incidents, however, either the local civil defence unit or the fire service are responsible for taking action. The emergency service personnel, however, usually only receive a general training in the action to be taken in the event of an emergency. Although some personnel may receive training in chemical hazards and the handling of dangerous substances, no specific hazardous waste training is given.

In Denmark, the employees of the Civil Defence Organisation receive very extensive and appropriate training for the management of chemical accidents and emergencies.

6.6 Conclusions and Recommendations

6.6.1 Conclusions

- Some degree of co-ordination of the emergency services exists in several Member States.

- Medical and nursing staff are rarely involved at incidents unless as members of a works medical section attending a site incident. Works medical officers usually have some training in industrial medicine and toxicology. Medical and nursing staff in hospitals are less likely to be specifically trained to respond to injuries arising from exposure to hazardous substances and wastes.

- Most fire services provide some information on hazardous substances within their standard training programmes, although the degree to which this is done depends on whether the trainees are professional or voluntary firemen. Generally more detailed training in this area is given to more senior staff. A number of fire services are establishing data banks to which reference can be made in the case of incidents involving hazardous substances. There is very little training in the specific problems associated with hazardous wastes.

- Police training in the subject varies again, depending on the role of the police and the degree of training they undergo. Such training as there is is usually rudimentary and tends to deal with hazardous substances in general, rather than wastes in particular. The main exceptions to this are the Netherlands, where environmental and wastes training is available, and the UK, where County Constabularies organise officer training relating to the transportation of hazardous wastes and dangerous goods.

- In Belgium, Denmark, Luxembourg and Spain, Civil Defence units have an important role to play in emergency situations. While some limited training in respect of hazardous products is given, there is no specific training in hazardous wastes.

6.6.2 Recommendations

The following paragraphs summarise the specific recommendations made by individual countries.

- Courses on hazardous wastes should be included in the training of personnel in the various emergency services wherever these are lacking: considerable emphasis should be placed on the practical aspects of dealing with such wastes in a emergency situation

- Greater co-operation should be encouraged between firms generating, transporting and disposing of hazardous wastes and the fire and medical services.

7.0 CONCLUSIONS AND RECOMMENDATIONS

7.1 Introduction

One of the recommendations of the European Round Table on Safety Aspects of Hazardous Wastes focused on the need for adequate education and training of all personnel involved in the handling and management of hazardous wastes, whether management or operatives. The principal purpose of this work has been to provide a detailed analysis of existing training provision, to identify the gaps and needs, and to put forward appropriate recommendations.

There are four main aims of the work:

- to provide a comprehensive picture and a comparative analysis of existing and planned education and training facilities in relation to hazardous wastes;

- to identify and analyse the educational and training needs of specific categories of personnel and of professionals dealing with problems relating to hazardous wastes, and to illustrate present shortcomings;

- to review successful training programmes and to encourage better and more extensive educational and training schemes for all relevant personnel both by pointing to improvements and by the exchange of information;

- to identify ways of improving both safety standards and possible remedial action in relation to hazardous wastes.

The study has addressed these objectives under a number of different headings. Each of the sections 2.0-6.0 summarises the education and training of personnel in different sectors: hazardous waste facilities, the transportation sector, those involved in the clean-up of contaminated soil, the regulatory agencies, and the emergency services. The conclusions and recommendations from each section are summarised below.

7.2 Findings of the study

7.2.1 Education and training of personnel working at hazardous waste facilities

Member States have passed very little legislation concerning the background and educational level required of those involved in the handling and treatment of hazardous wastes. The main stipulations for most countries are that managers and responsible persons must be appropriately qualified, although specific qualifications are not normally stipulated.

In practice, the educational level of management and supervisory personnel is high. Managers are typically educated to at least degree and diploma level, usually in chemistry or chemical engineering. To some extent, however, the level of qualification demanded will depend on the level of technical complexity of the facility under consideration. Chemical waste incineration plants demand high level qualifications of their management and supervisory staff, while landfill sites in several countries are often supervised by staff with little more than basic school education plus some relevant work experience.

Most operatives have completed little more than basic schooling, and have not received any prior training in the handling of hazardous wastes. Furthermore, the length of schooling varies to some extent from country to country. Some of the workers in one Portuguese plant were found to have completed only four years of schooling. In the more sophisticated plants, operatives may have attended day-release courses or completed apprenticeships.

There is little statutory provision for training in the handling and management of hazardous wastes. Most countries rely on existing health and safety legislation to protect the interests of employees.

Actual training provision therefore varies considerably between Member States. A high proportion of training, particularly in the area of health and safety at work is undertaken in-house by the companies concerned. Opportunities for operative training externally are the exception rather than the rule, although management and supervisory staff are encouraged to take advantage of seminars and conferences on relevant topics where these are available. To some extent training reflects the structure of the industry. Where hazardous waste facilities are small-scale and widely scattered, small staff numbers and the cost of training restricts both the development of internal and attendance at external courses. In countries such as France, where hazardous waste treatment is concentrated in the hands of a small number of large organisations, training can be more effectively organised.

The number of relevant external training courses is limited. In general, those countries with a longer experience of handling hazardous wastes can offer a greater number and variety of relevant courses. A major gap identified in various countries was the need for appropriate refresher courses.

There would appear to be major opportunities for the development of training in countries such as Spain and Greece where training provision is virtually non-existent, and also in other countries where the structure of the industry, or of sections of the industry, hinders the development of training schemes.

7.2.2 Education and training of personnel involved in the transportation of hazardous wastes

Road Transport

Road transport is more frequently used than any other form of transport for the transportation of hazardous wastes.

The educational background of most drivers is limited to basic school education plus, occasionally, some vocational training. Most drivers employed have some experience of driving. Member States usually stipulate training requirements for drivers of vehicles transporting hazardous substances. Sometimes this is for tanker drivers only: in other cases it covers all forms of hazardous goods transportation. All employers must also comply with national work safety legislation. At management level, the degree of educational qualification tends to vary with the size of the organisation.

Most Member States apart from Greece have some form of required driver training, and much of the training is either for or approximately equivalent to that required for the International ADR certificate. Both external and in-house courses are run for this purpose. However, nearly all such training relates to hazardous substances in general and there is little training relating to the specific problems of hazardous wastes. Recognising the need, a number of organisations and companies are beginning to develop appropriate training courses. Difficulties are experienced by the smaller firms in some countries because of the degree of competition, the costs of training and the cost of employing drivers with better qualifications.

Rail Transport

Rail transport is used to only a very limited extent in the transportation of hazardous wastes and none of the countries involved undertakes any training in the handling or management of hazardous wastes, although a limited degree of training on the carriage of dangerous goods in general does take place.

Sea Transport

There is no legislation on the educational qualifications required of those involved in the transportation of hazardous wastes, although Captains and Officers will have been trained to a certain minimum level. Neither is there any specific legislation regarding training for those involved in the transportation of hazardous wastes. Courses are available dealing with the handling of dangerous goods in general and Officer training usually incorporates some instruction in dangerous substances. German law does specify safety obligations when handling mixtures and solutions.

Transport by Inland Waterways

There are no specific requirements regarding the education and training of those involved in the transportation of hazardous wastes by inland waterway. Such transportation would be covered by the various items of legislation concerning hazardous goods in general.

7.2.3 Education and training of personnel involved in the clean-up of contaminated soil

Very few Member States have an accurate inventory of sites contaminated with hazardous wastes.

Most clean-up of contaminated sites results from accidents and the need to take emergency action. Only six Member States are directly involved in the clean-up of contaminated soil to any significant extent.

The management and supervisory staff involved are normally qualified to the equivalent of degree level, the levels required depending to some extent on the degree of hazard involved. Operatives have normally only completed the basic school education. Furthermore, there is no statutory obligation to provide training for those working on the clean-up of contaminated land, although national health and safety regulations apply for the protection of employees.

Denmark and the Netherlands both offer courses on working with contaminated land. In Germany and the UK, most training takes place on the job, although Loughborough University in the UK does offer a relevant advanced course. Smet-Jet in Belgium has developed its own sophisticated in-house training scheme. Most of the external courses available are geared to middle and senior management.

7.2.4 Education and training in relation to the duties and responsibilities of regulatory agencies

Those organisations responsible for administering and monitoring the standards applied to the management of hazardous waste are clearly defined in most Member States. However, in Germany and Greece, monitoriing is complicated by the division of responsibility between large numbers of different departments.

In most Member States a high proportion of those involved in inspection and monitoring the management of hazardous wastes are graduates or senior civil servants with qualifications in such subjects as chemistry, engineering and biology. This particularly applies to senior posts. In Germany, however, because of the large number of different departments responsible for this work, the number of personnel involved is substantial and their qualifications are varied.

Training provision varies from country to country. There are no statutory regulations regarding training in this area of work, but most countries accept the importance of training even if, in practice, this is restricted to training on the job. There is no systematic training in issues relating to hazardous wastes for staff in any Member State. However, external courses which contain relevant elements are offered in most of the more industrialised countries. In addition, seminars or conferences on topics of relevance may be held.

The main problems encountered in the provision of appropriate training are the lack of resources (funds, qualified instructors, equipment etc), lack of an adequate infrastructure in certain Member States, and understaffing with its associated difficulties of releasing staff for training.

The main need is for appropriate courses to be developed.

7.2.5 Education and training of those in the emergency services in relation to hazardous wastes

Some degree of co-ordination of the emergency services does exist in several Member States.

Medical and nursing staff are rarely involved at incidents unless as members of a works medical section attending a site incident. Works medical officers usually have some training in industrial medicine and toxicology. Medical and nursing staff in hospitals are less likely to be specifically trained to respond to injuries arising from exposure to hazardous substances and wastes.

Most fire services provide some information on hazardous substances within their standard training programmes, although the degree to which this is done depends on whether the trainees are professional or voluntary firemen. Generally more detailed training in this area is given to more senior staff. A number of fire services are establishing data banks to which reference can be made in the case of incidents involving hazardous substances. There is very little training in the specific problems associated with hazardous wastes.

Police training in the subject varies again, depending on the role of the police and the degree of training they undergo. Such training as there is is usually rudimentary and tends to deal with hazardous substances in general, rather than wastes in particular. The main exceptions to this are the Netherlands, where environmental and wastes training is available, and the UK, where County Constabularies organise officer training relating to the transportation of hazardous wastes and dangerous goods.

In Belgium, Luxembourg and Spain, Civil Defence units have an important role to play in emergency situations. While some limited training in respect of hazardous products is given, there is no specific training in hazardous wastes.

7.2.6 Other Conclusions

While the study has focused on the training issues and needs of personnel involved in the disposal aspects of hazardous waste management, it is also important that employees working in industries that generate hazardous wastes have access to relevant training courses and receive appropriate supervision from qualified staff on the handling and management of hazardous wastes.

Management and technical staff should also have the opportunity to examine the potential for the introduction of measures which may lead to an overall reduction in the volume of hazardous waste generated, for example, through the use of clean technologies and the design of environmentally friendly products. In this respect there may be a need for additional training or instruction, perhaps through case study examples (particularly for SME's), which illustrate the potential for waste prevention and minimisation.

Finally, in addition to formal training and education, there are a number of computerised data systems available within the Community which provide information on issues related to the management of hazardous waste. For example, in the UK there is a hazardous substances data bank operated by Harwell Laboratory which provides information on the physical and chemical properties of hazardous substances and the appropriate methods of control in case of accidents. Another example is the ISPRA data bank in Italy, on risk prevention and analysis, which is concerned with anticipating and predicting impacts arising from accidents involving hazardous substances.

7.3 Recommendations

The following paragraphs summarise, under each main heading, the recommendations made in the individual national reports.

7.3.1 Education and training of personnel working at hazardous waste facilities

There should be some degree of standardisation of qualification requirements for special waste disposal facilities.

Every firm should appoint an officer with specific responsibility for the environment.

Countries lacking any basic training facilities should establish a basic training programme and possibly a training centre.

All courses in environmental sciences and techniques, wherever located, should consider the question of hazardous wastes in greater detail.

Every firm should develop appropriate training programmes.

More courses (with practical demonstrations) on properties of chemicals and their toxicity should be developed.

There should be more training in the operation of incinerators and other specialised waste facilities.

There should be more professional qualifications in waste management particularly in the landfill sector and for certain other workers, eg incinerator operators.

7.3.2 Education and training of personnel involved in the transportation of hazardous wastes

Training courses specifically geared to the transportation of hazardous wastes should be developed.

Co-operation in training should be encouraged.

Drivers should be retrained at intervals of less than five years to allow regular updating: training on hazardous wastes should be included in normal ADR training

A professional profile should be established for specialist waste-disposal heavy goods drivers.

7.3.3 Education and training of personnel involved in the clean-up of contaminated soil

More training provision is needed for 'shop-floor' personnel.

Additional courses are required at the decision-making level.

More practical training is needed to provide a better knowledge of chemicals.

7.3.4 Education and training in relation to the duties and responsibilities of regulatory agencies

The following paragraphs summarise the specific recommendations made by individual countries.

- Training should be improved, particularly in terms of knowledge of legislation, administrative and judiciary procedures of wastes management and safety. Resources therefore need to be made available.

- There is a need for more specialist waste management courses to be developed in order to ensure responsible officers are kept up to date on technological developments affecting the nature and generation of industrial waste and on new developments within the waste disposal industry.

- Regional co-ordination of training should take place where appropriate in order to encourage participation and reduce costs.

- Resources for setting up and participating in training corses on hazardous wastes need to be made available.

7.3.5 Education and training of those in the emergency services in relation to hazardous wastes

Courses on hazardous wastes should be included in the training of personnel in the various emergency services wherever these are lacking: considerable emphasis should be placed on the practical aspects of dealing with such wastes in an emergency situation

Greater co-operation should be encouraged between firms generating, transporting, and disposing of hazardous wastes and the fire and medical services.

ANNEX I: EXAMPLES OF COURSES AND AGENCIES PROVIDING TRAINING ON ASPECTS OF HAZARDOUS WASTE MANAGEMENT

BELGIUM

CRESEPT - "Training in the Management of hazardous substances and wastes", (CRESEPT - Centre for Study and Research and Safety, Ergonomics and the Promotion of Working Conditions).

FRANCE

INRS - National Institute for Research and Safety, organises courses for hazardous waste producers.

INSA - National Institute for Applied Sciences, Lyon, offers a diploma in the treatment and management of wastes.

IGGE - International Institute of Environmental Management and Engineering, Aix les Bains (Savoie).

GERMANY

Waste Technician - North Rhein Wetphalia Berufsschule für Landesfachklassen Gelselsenkirchen, Stadt. Schule der Sekundärstufe II, Heegestraße 14, 4650 Gelsenkirchen.

Waste Technician - Gelsenkirche Fachschule für Technik Fachrichtung Abfalltechnik.

- "The Waste Disposal Specialist", Haus der Technik, Essen.

- "Special Waste, Legal Principles, Disposal Procedures, Analyses, Waste Type, Classification", Technische Akademie, Wuppertal.

- "Transportation of Hazardous Wastes", Dekra Akademie, Stuttgart.

- "Planning of Waste Treatment Plant", Technische Universität, Berlin.

- "Processing Industrial and Special Wastes", RKW, Berlin.

- Training in waste handling, collection, storage and disposal - range of courses at VDI-Bildungswerk GmbH, Düsseldorf.

UNITED KINGDOM

Loughborough University - Diploma in Hazardous Waste Management, Loughborough Centre for Extension Studies.

Institute of Waste Management - Diploma in Waste Management, IWM, Nottingham.

European Communities — Commission

The Education and Training of Personnel Involved in the Handling and Monitoring of Hazardous Wastes

Luxembourg: Office for Official Publications of the European Communities

1992 — 70 pp. — 16 x 23.5 cm

ISBN 92-826-3998-3

Price (excluding VAT) in Luxembourg: ECU 7.50

**Venta y suscripciones • Salg og abonnement • Verkauf und Abonnement • Πωλήσεις και συνδρομές
Sales and subscriptions • Vente et abonnements • Vendita e abbonamenti
Verkoop en abonnementen • Venda e assinaturas**

BELGIQUE / BELGIË

Moniteur belge /
Belgisch Staatsblad
Rue de Louvain 42 / Leuvenseweg 42
1000 Bruxelles / 1000 Brussel
Tél. (02) 512 00 26
Fax 511 01 84
CCP / Postrekening 000-2005502-27

Autres distributeurs /
Overige verkooppunten

Librairie européenne/
Europese Boekhandel
Avenue Albert Jonnart 50 /
Albert Jonnartlaan 50
1200 Bruxelles / 1200 Brussel
Tél. (02) 734 02 81
Fax 735 08 60

Jean De Lannoy
Avenue du Roi 202 /Koningslaan 202
1060 Bruxelles / 1060 Brussel
Tél. (02) 538 51 69
Télex 63220 UNBOOK B
Fax (02) 538 08 41

CREDOC
Rue de la Montagne 34 / Bergstraat 34
Bte 11 / Bus 11
1000 Bruxelles / 1000 Brussel

DANMARK

J. H. Schultz Information A/S
EF-Publikationer
Ottiliavej 18
2500 Valby
Tlf. 36 44 22 66
Fax 36 44 01 41
Girokonto 6 00 08 86

BR DEUTSCHLAND

Bundesanzeiger Verlag
Breite Straße
Postfach 10 80 06
5000 Köln 1
Tel. (02 21) 20 29-0
Telex ANZEIGER BONN 8 882 595
Fax 20 29 278

GREECE/ΕΛΛΑΔΑ

G.C. Eleftheroudakis SA
International Bookstore
Nikis Street 4
10563 Athens
Tel. (01) 322 63 23
Telex 219410 ELEF
Fax 323 98 21

ESPAÑA

Boletín Oficial del Estado
Trafalgar, 27
28010 Madrid
Tel. (91) 44 82 135

Mundi-Prensa Libros, S.A.
Castelló, 37
28001 Madrid
Tel. (91) 431 33 99 (Libros)
     431 32 22 (Suscripciones)
     435 36 37 (Dirección)
Télex 49370-MPLI-E
Fax (91) 575 39 98

Sucursal:

Librería Internacional AEDOS
Consejo de Ciento, 391
08009 Barcelona
Tel. (93) 301 86 15
Fax (93) 317 01 41

Llibreria de la Generalitat
de Catalunya
Rambla dels Estudis, 118 (Palau Moja)
08002 Barcelona
Tel. (93) 302 68 35
    302 64 62
Fax (93) 302 12 99

FRANCE

Journal officiel
Service des publications
des Communautés européennes
26, rue Desaix
75727 Paris Cedex 15
Tél. (1) 40 58 75 00
Fax (1) 40 58 75 74

IRELAND

Government Supplies Agency
4-5 Harcourt Road
Dublin 2
Tel. (1) 61 31 11
Fax (1) 78 06 45

ITALIA

Licosa Spa
Via Duca di Calabria, 1/1
Casella postale 552
50125 Firenze
Tel. (055) 64 54 15
Fax 64 12 57
Telex 570466 LICOSA I
CCP 343 509

GRAND-DUCHÉ DE LUXEMBOURG

Messageries Paul Kraus
11, rue Christophe Plantin
2339 Luxembourg
Tél. 499 88 88
Télex 2515
Fax 499 88 84 44
CCP 49242-63

NEDERLAND

SDU Overheidsinformatie
Externe Fondsen
Postbus 20014
2500 EA 's-Gravenhage
Tel. (070) 37 89 911
Fax (070) 34 75 778

PORTUGAL

Imprensa Nacional
Casa da Moeda, EP
Rua D. Francisco Manuel de Melo, 5
1092 Lisboa Codex
Tel. (01) 69 34 14

Distribuidora de Livros
Bertrand, Ld.ª
Grupo Bertrand, SA
Rua das Terras dos Vales, 4-A
Apartado 37
2700 Amadora Codex
Tel. (01) 49 59 050
Telex 15798 BERDIS
Fax 49 60 255

UNITED KINGDOM

HMSO Books (PC 16)
HMSO Publications Centre
51 Nine Elms Lane
London SW8 5DR
Tel. (071) 873 2000
Fax GP3 873 8463
Telex 29 71 138

ÖSTERREICH

Manz'sche Verlags-
und Universitätsbuchhandlung
Kohlmarkt 16
1014 Wien
Tel. (0222) 531 61-0
Telex 11 25 00 BOX A
Fax (0222) 531 61-39

SUOMI

Akateeminen Kirjakauppa
Keskuskatu 1
PO Box 128
00101 Helsinki
Tel. (0) 121 41
Fax (0) 121 44 41

NORGE

Narvesen information center
Bertrand Narvesens vei 2
PO Box 6125 Etterstad
0602 Oslo 6
Tel. (2) 57 33 00
Telex 79668 NIC N
Fax (2) 68 19 01

SVERIGE

BTJ
Box 200
22100 Lund
Tel. (046) 18 00 00
Fax (046) 18 01 25

SCHWEIZ / SUISSE / SVIZZERA

OSEC
Stampfenbachstraße 85
8035 Zürich
Tel. (01) 365 54 49
Fax (01) 365 54 11

CESKOSLOVENSKO

NIS
Havelkova 22
13000 Praha 3
Tel. (02) 235 84 46
Fax 42-2-264775

MAGYARORSZÁG

Euro-Info-Service
Budapest I. Kir.
Attila út 93
1012 Budapest
Tel. (1) 56 82 11
Telex (22) 4717 AGINF H-61
Fax (1) 17 59 031

POLSKA

Business Foundation
ul. Krucza 38/42
00-512 Warszawa
Tel. (22) 21 99 93, 628-28-82
International Fax&Phone
(0-39) 12-00-77

JUGOSLAVIJA

Privredni Vjesnik
Bulevar Lenjina 171/XIV
11070 Beograd
Tel. (11) 123 23 40

CYPRUS

Cyprus Chamber of Commerce and
Industry
Chamber Building
38 Grivas Dhigenis Ave
3 Deligiorgis Street
PO Box 1455
Nicosia
Tel. (2) 449500/462312
Fax (2) 458630

TÜRKIYE

Pres Gazete Kitap Dergi
Pazarlama Daǧitim Ticaret ve sanayi
AŞ
Narlibahçe Sokak N. 15
Istanbul-Caǧaloǧlu
Tel. (1) 520 92 96 - 528 55 66
Fax 520 64 57
Telex 23822 DSVO-TR

CANADA

Renouf Publishing Co. Ltd
Mail orders — Head Office:
1294 Algoma Road
Ottawa, Ontario K1B 3W8
Tel. (613) 741 43 33
Fax (613) 741 54 39
Telex 0534783

Ottawa Store:
61 Sparks Street
Tel. (613) 238 89 85

Toronto Store:
211 Yonge Street
Tel. (416) 363 31 71

UNITED STATES OF AMERICA

UNIPUB
4611-F Assembly Drive
Lanham, MD 20706-4391
Tel. Toll Free (800) 274 4888
Fax (301) 459 0056

AUSTRALIA

Hunter Publications
58A Gipps Street
Collingwood
Victoria 3066

JAPAN

Kinokuniya Company Ltd
17-7 Shinjuku 3-Chome
Shinjuku-ku
Tokyo 160-91
Tel. (03) 3439-0121

Journal Department
PO Box 55 Chitose
Tokyo 156
Tel. (03) 3439-0124

**AUTRES PAYS
OTHER COUNTRIES
ANDERE LÄNDER**

Office des publications officielles
des Communautés européennes
2, rue Mercier
2985 Luxembourg
Tél. 49 92 81
Télex PUBOF LU 1324 b
Fax 48 85 73/48 68 17
CC bancaire BIL 8-109/6003/700

12/91